You'll Never Beat Way

Ten Year Testimonial Book

Edited by Ian Jackson

London League Publications Ltd
on behalf of the Wayne English Testimonial

**You'll Never Beat Wayne English
Ten Year Testimonial Book**

© Articles copyright to the contributors.

The moral right of the contributors to be identified as the authors has been asserted.

Cover design © Marj Collaco. Photographs © Pete Green. Paintings © John Prince. Poems © John Spellman. No copyright has been infringed intentionally.

This book is copyright under the Berne Convention. All rights reserved.

A CIP catalogue record of this book is available from the British Library.

Front cover photograph: Wayne English attacks the line with Marlon Billy in support against Locomotiv Moscow in a Challenge Cup match at Park Lane on 13 March 2005.
Back cover photograph: Wayne English somersaults as he scores a vital try against Hunslet Hawks in a National League Two match at Park Lane on 3 August 2008.
Title page photograph: Wayne English attempts to evade a would be Russian tackler against Locomotiv Moscow in a Challenge Cup match at Park Lane on 13 March 2005.

Published by London League Publications Limited, PO Box 10441, London E14 8WR on behalf of the Wayne English Testimonial.

The Wayne English Testimonial Committee would like to thank all the contributors, the Swinton Lions Supporters' Trust and London League Publications Ltd for their help in preparing this book.

ISBN: 978-1903659-45-8

Lay-out: Ian Jackson

Printed and bound in Wiltshire, England by CPI Antony Rowe Limited

This book is dedicated to the family and friends of Wayne English and to all the loyal supporters of Swinton Lions Rugby League Football Club.

Foreword

A testimonial in rugby league is a great honour. It is awarded only to players who have shown great loyalty to a club or the game. Wayne English deserves his testimonial because he has demonstrated his loyalty to Swinton over and over again. Wayne and I have much in common even though he signed for the Lions 25 years after I retired. We are both full-backs with strong Rochdale connections and are loyal Swinton players who have been awarded testimonials.

The art of a full-back requires many skills to master. Positional sense is vital, tackling is essential and an attacking prowess is required along with a good dose of bravery. What marks Wayne out as a good full-back in the modern game is that he uses possession of the football as an attacking feature and he is always seeking to exploit gaps often early in the tackle count. The six-tackle rule was introduced part way through my career and although I didn't like it at first I came to realise that you have to build attacks immediately and this is what Wayne does as soon as he gathers possession from a kick.

Wayne is a Rochdale lad and I'm sure Hornets would have benefited from his presence in their colours. My father, Walter Gowers, was a Rochdale Hornets player from 1922 and he toured Australia and New Zealand in 1928 with Great Britain. He still holds many Rochdale club records including points in a season, points in a career and most career appearances. Some of these club records I hold for the Lions and I also followed in my father's footsteps when I toured down under in 1966.

During my career with Swinton, I was fortunate to have two testimonials since I was with the Lions from 1954 to 1973 during the great days of back-to-back championships at Station Road. I played when players did not transfer between clubs as often as today. So for Wayne to stay with Swinton through some troubled times is a credit to him and his loyalty.

What's fascinating about Wayne's career is how he signed for the club and then began learning his trade as a full-back in the professional game playing in the academy. He didn't change position or switch clubs. Wayne was given his chance at Swinton and set about working to establish himself in the first team. This is how young players made a name for themselves in my day. It's a proven path going back to when my father played and for Wayne it's been successful. Finally, I would like to wish Wayne every success with his benefit and all the best for the rest of his career, hopefully like me, at Swinton.

Ken Gowers
Swinton RLFC 1954 to 1973 and Great Britain 1962 to 1966

Introduction to Swinton's number one

A career spanning 10 years at Swinton Lions RLFC is testimony to the character of Wayne English. The Lions are no longer a glamour club or even relatively successful and Wayne has no actual connection to the area on any level. He was not born in Swinton and has never lived in the town. So the loyalty shown by him to a club that has had bouts of profound crisis during his playing career deserves wider recognition. Since the start of the new millennium, everyone at Swinton knows who you mean when you talk about Wayne, because he has been a consistent performer in the blue and white shirt.

This book tells the story of a talented rugby league player from Rochdale before and during his career at Swinton. To see Wayne English carrying the ball in full flight; or completing a last-ditch cover tackle has been truly marvellous on many occasions. He is both athletic and agile in the toughest sport imaginable. And then to see him with his family or talking to supporters in the clubhouse after the game is equally inspiring. He is a genuine sportsman in every sense of the word. However, the book does not mark the end of his career similar to many others written about professional sportsmen. It captures simply a moment in time 10 years after he signed as a teenager from the amateur club Kirkholt. The book attempts to spotlight a rugby league player outside Super League and beyond the usual media gaze. It sets in context the game and its environment and shows that loyalty can flourish even in the most difficult of places.

This is the third book written exclusively about Swinton Lions RLFC and the first to be based on the career of a single player. The aim of the book is to mark the testimonial of Wayne English and also capture a decade of events at Swinton Lions since the publication of the complete history of the club by Steve Wild in 1999. This book contains a foreword by Swinton and Great Britain legend Ken Gowers as well as first hand accounts of events from players, coaches, officials and supporters alike who have witnessed some monumental changes at the club.

Wayne English Testimonial Committee
Swinton and Pendlebury
March, 2009

A message

I would like to thank you for buying a copy of my Testimonial book, which is intended to record recent events at Swinton Lions RLFC. I regard myself as a Swinton supporter and reminisce over the previous decade with great pride. It is 10 years since I signed for the Lions from Kirkholt WMC, a team based in my hometown of Rochdale. At the beginning, I joined the academy team managed by John Prince and since breaking into the first-team against Waterhead in the Challenge Cup in February 2000 I have continued to enjoy my time as a Swinton Lions player.

The late Mike Gregory handed me my debut and I have been coached by other influential figures including Les Holliday, Phil Veivers, Peter Roe and Paul Kidd. I have also played in the same Swinton team with some outstanding players such as Marlon Billy, Peter Cannon, Andy Coley, Simon Knox, Mick Nanyn, Jason Roach and Ian Watson.

I would like to acknowledge the contribution to this book by Ken Gowers who wrote the foreword, John Prince for creating the paintings, Pete Green for the photographs and John Spellman for the poem. In addition, my thanks go to Brent Andrews, Tony Appleyard, Marlon Billy, Norman Brown, Peter Cannon, Paul Kidd, Vinny Kirkman, Simon Mather, Claire Mooney, Jason Roach, Colin Robinson, Richard Taylor, John Thomason and Jeff Tyldesley. Also, thanks to the many people who subscribed to the book and in particular, I would like to make a special mention of Graham Berry, a life-long Swinton supporter, who subscribed but sadly passed away in early 2009.

Finally, I want to show my appreciation to the many people who have helped me with my rugby league career, including my family and friends plus all the Swinton fans for making me feel an important part of the club over the years. I would like to thank you all for your support with my Testimonial.

Wayne English
Rochdale
March, 2009

Our "Jack Russell"

I am proud and honoured to be asked to write about Wayne English for his Testimonial book. As the Swinton Lions RLFC development manager in the 1990s, I was instrumental in bringing Wayne to the club in July 1998. I am going to tell you some interesting things about Wayne, but first a few words of context about my experiences.

Believe it or not, a decade ago on 11 August 1999 (Eclipses Day) I was getting up to go to work as rugby league development manager with Swinton Lions. This was the best and most enjoyable job of my life since I was getting paid to do something I love. On that fateful day, I fell down stairs when the carpet came away. I tumbled doing a somersault at the bottom breaking my neck in two places (C6 and C7). I dislocated another vertebra and sustained several less serious injuries including breaking my fingers and right knee cap.

After a nightmare hospital experience that would take another book of its own to describe, I returned four and a half weeks later to the hospital. At this point I had been unable to lie down and slept when I could, usually in a chair at the side of the bed. I was in the worst pain I have ever had in my life. After another 10 days, I was sent to have a scan when the full extent of my injuries became apparent for the first time.

I still can't feel my arms and legs. I am in constant pain 24 hours a day, 7 days a week. I can only describe the pain as constant toothache down my arms and legs or banging your funny bone. Despite these problems following 12 months of hospitalization as well as a real fight for life, (living on high dependency wards, with other people also fighting for their lives) I am able to pass on my beliefs and at the same time keep myself positive. I am still alive and I am able to write a tribute about Wayne English.

It brings back fond memories to remember a 17-year old player I spotted playing full-back for Kirkholt Working Men's Club in 1997. I was quite excited as I watched this young man who could step-off either foot and who had genuine pace. Also, he had a heart as big as a lion typified by a tremendous tackling technique. Many said he was too small for the professional game, but I disagreed saying that if you're good enough then you're big enough.

I began working for Swinton Lions after being brought in by Tony Barrow, who was the first-team coach at the time. We go back a long way as players at Leigh RLFC and officials of the North West Counties Rugby League youth leagues mainly as opposing coaches. Tony had asked me to establish an academy side at Swinton, which I did. The side lost only one game in its first season. More importantly the 'A' team also gained promotion that season after finishing bottom the year before. It was good to witness the academy players moving-up quickly into the ranks of the reserve team and beyond. In total, four academy players made their first-team debuts that initial season.

After spotting Wayne, I arranged to meet him and his father Mick and although I knew that other clubs including Halifax, Keighley and Rochdale Hornets were also interested in his signature, I managed to persuade them both that Swinton at the time offered the quickest way into first-team rugby.

The rest is history and it is good to be able to see 10 years later that Wayne still displays the same skills that I first saw when I found him all those years ago in Rochdale. More importantly he is the only player from that era who still plays for the Lions. The following is a list of players, who like Wayne English, began their professional career with Swinton Lions:

Martin Gleeson: Huddersfield, St Helens, Warrington, England and Great Britain
Andy Coley: Salford, Wigan and England
Paul Smith: Rochdale Hornets, Huddersfield and Halifax
Lee Doran: Oldham, Widnes and Leigh
David Newton: Oldham and Rochdale Hornets
Phil Cushion: Celtic Crusaders
Mick Nanyn: Whitehaven, Widnes, Rochdale Hornets, Oldham, Harlequins RL and Scotland

As you can see, Wayne English was part of an exciting set-up. So much so that Martin Gleeson and Andy Coley have gained international honours for Great Britain and England, respectively; and Mick Nanyn has played in the Rugby League World Cup for Scotland.

There are other players from that era, many of whom played in the Swinton first-team and who have also developed their careers after the Lions. This second list includes players who have either finished playing after spells with other professional clubs or are still playing at the amateur level. The players are John McMullen - who represented the Great Britain Rugby League amateur side - Damien Cleary, Ryan Stazicker, Wesley Else, Kenny Nicholson, Chris Flynn, Mark Bolton, David McComas, Anthony Robinson, Phil Robinson, Alan Walsh, Bob Whittaker, David Myers, James Prior, Paul Brett, Craig Eccleston, James Watt, James Morris and Peter Green. If the Lions had not fallen on hard times then what a side they could have had over the years.

Above all else, this demonstrates the loyalty Wayne English has given to the Lions. I know for a fact that Wayne, like all the others, had the potential to move to another club and that other clubs have been interested in signing him.

The list includes Rochdale Hornets, Widnes and Castleford to name a few. I also believe that Wayne could have made the grade at a higher level with the great talents he possesses. This is the main reason to applaud Wayne's loyalty and support him in his testimonial.

In July 2008, I was invited to give a little speech at Wayne's testimonial launch night dinner. I was greatly honoured to do so for a player who so richly deserves a good testimonial. At that dinner, I met Peter Whelan, the Lions video camera operator. Peter and Richard Taylor asked me if I wanted to commentate on the Lions next game. I accepted the offer and have fulfilled this role until the end of the 2008 season. I have thoroughly enjoyed the experience and once again enjoyed meeting all the very loyal Swinton Lions fans.

It was the most enjoyable of times being able to watch our "Jack Russell" also known as Wayne English once more, who is still bringing excitement to the team with his try-saving and try-scoring exploits. I know that it has been a disappointing season in 2008 but I urge everyone to support Wayne's testimonial and make every effort to tell lapsed fans how much this player has given to the Swinton Lions.

After my accident and subsequent operations, I can no longer feel my arms and legs. I took up art as a therapy to learn how to use my arms again. I went to collage and in 2002 I achieved the NCEFE North West of England student of the year. I have produced two 20 inch by 16 inch framed graphite drawings of Wayne and another two 20 inch by 16 inch framed pastel paintings of him. I have donated these originals pictures to Wayne's Testimonial fund and there are also prints available for sale including the two contained in this book.

To Wayne, his partner Nina, daughter Alicia, mum Denise and father Mike and all his family and friends, I would like to wish everyone all the best for this testimonial season. I am pleased to say how important it is supporting a very worthy young man in what has been an incredible 10 years with the Lions.

Finally, to the Lions fans who Wayne and I rate among the best in the game, even though there are fewer numbers recently, I'd like to say keep positive, enjoy the game, live each day and support this young man who has contributed to the history of this famous club.

Come on you Lions.

John Prince
Leigh
September 2008

The view from the Physio

I have been at Swinton over 30 years in various roles, mainly as the club physiotherapist. I have seen at first hand all the outstanding players at the club and shared with them many laughs on the training ground or on the team coach travelling to and from away games. There have been some really great players at Swinton; some at the start of a career in rugby league and others towards the end. I can honestly say that I knew Wayne English was full of potential as soon as he arrived and it's really pleasing to see he has be awarded a testimonial ten years later.

My initial recollection of Wayne when he arrived at Swinton was most favourable. I was very impressed with his electric pace which I knew would cause problems for opposing defences. I soon realised that he's a very tough little player as well. At first, some of the bigger players in teams we played against would target Wayne and run at him hoping to knock him out of the way. Let me tell you very few ever did and he nearly always made the tackle. Mind you, Wayne would often field the ball and then run down the line looking for the biggest opposing player to run at himself. We soon had to put a stop to that as other teams got wise to it and in any case it was a daft thing to do.

In a game, Wayne can be really laid back. He can amble to collect the ball kicked over the top of the Lions defence, but not because he's stalling or playing for time. It's because he is full of confidence and knows he has the pace to deal with most situations. He could show more urgency from time to time, but that's Wayne, I suppose and always will be, I'm sure. One time he did show too much urgency was in a match at London Skolars in 2003. A fight erupted and Wayne steamed in, clocking one particular London player and was promptly sent off. After the game, I asked him what it was all about and apparently Wayne got a really good view of Phil Cushion taking a couple of punches and was simply standing-up for a team-mate.

It is well known that Wayne can show a lot of bravery even though he can be too brave for his own good at times. In 2008 at Workington, he made a tackle and I saw him recover from the impact more slowly than he does usually. Anyway, he carried on playing and after the game he said: "I think I've broken my jaw." So, I sent him to hospital and sure enough the X-ray confirmed the worst. He was back by the end of the season and not only that but he was playing his very best rugby for the Lions again. That's bravery for you.

Wayne has quite a dry sense of humour although he is not cheeky or a practical joker, like some of the players can be from time-to-time. Often he makes a wisecrack and it is not heard in the general noise of the changing room. Many people don't realise that Danny Wilson also had quite a dry sense of humour in his Swinton days; although it is true Danny could often take things too far. On one occasion during a return journey from an away game in the early 1980s, Tom Grainey, the Swinton coach at the time, had fallen asleep as he was prone to do. One of the players squirted shaving foam all over the top of his head, but this was not enough for Danny who placed several matches upright on top and then lit them all. Everyone around began to sing *Happy Birthday* and the startled Tom awoke and joined in the singing momentarily until he realised what had happened.

Wayne's humour is usually more subtle. I remember one occasion before an important game at Oldham. The changing room was tense and a little nervous as the kick-off approached. Normally players know to turn off mobile telephones straight away and most do as a matter of course. Les Holliday was conducting the pre-match team-talk and was working hard getting the players to focus. Everyone was sat down listening intently to Les, an experienced former Great Britain loose forward and someone who knows the game inside-out. Suddenly, Les was interrupted by the ring-tone of a mobile telephone. Les stopped talking and then Wayne reached up and answers his 'phone. He muttered a few words like "yes" and "alright" and then ends the call. Les asked him "What was that?" and as quick as flash Wayne answered "Tactics Les, tactics." The whole place erupted with laughter and although Les didn't say anything there and then to Wayne, I'm pretty sure he did later when the right opportunity arose.

Finally, I have been asked from time-to-time why Wayne has avoided many injuries that can ruin a playing career in the game. From my viewpoint, it's easy to tell you why Wayne is not injury prone. It's because he's a tough player and brave with it, too. In fact, Wayne is no trouble at all. He has both thumbs strapped before a game and that's it. He's as good as gold and we've never had a cross word other than telling him that he can't always do the spectacular. That's Wayne, for you though. He can do the spectacular and he is so committed to Swinton that he wants to do it every time he has the ball in his hands.

Norman Brown
Swinton and Pendlebury
October 2008

Contents

1.	The early years and signing professional	1
2.	The first five years: 1999 to 2003	9
3.	The second five years: 2004 to 2008	33
4.	The future and reflections on a professional	55
5.	Swinton full-backs since 1866	65
6.	Tributes and the fans' zone	73

References   99

Appendices   100

    A. Wayne English summary from 2000 to 2008
    B. Swinton Lions summary from 1999 to 2008
    C. Swinton Lions match-by-match from 1999 to 2008
    D. Swinton Lions player-by-player from 1999 to 2008
    E. Whatever happened to 13 Swinton players?
    F. Wayne English's top ten matches
    G. Wayne English's Swinton Lions XIII: 1999 to 2008
    H. Wayne English's All-time World XIII: 1999 to 2008

Subscribers   138

Wayne English by John Prince (2008)

1. The early years and signing professional

"It brings back fond memories to remember a 17-year old player I spotted playing full-back for Kirkholt Working Men's Club in 1997. I was quite excited as I watched this young man who could step-off either foot and who had genuine pace."
John Prince (2008) reflections on Wayne English

Introduction
Rugby league is an exceptionally demanding sport so much so that anyone who plays it has to be tough both physically and mentally. As a result, players at any level do not appear from nowhere and have to develop rigorously to learn the skills of the game often from being quite young. This is exactly what happened with Wayne English. He was schooled in the game from an early age, playing in the youth sections of local amateur clubs. Subsequently, he benefited from representing his home town team and then the county team while still at school before eventually turning professional. This is an account of the initial part of Wayne English's journey from a schoolboy and amateur playing the game for fun to becoming a professional and earning eventually a testimonial after 10 years.

Early days: born in the 1980s
Wayne English was born on 8 March 1980 in Rochdale. He is part of a close family including mum Denise, dad Mike and two older sisters Colleen and Christine. Wayne has always had the support of his parents and grandparents, which he has acknowledged as an important part of his success. Wayne grew up in Rochdale, a town which is famous as the birthplace of the Co-operative movement as well as nurturing great national personalities such as entertainer Gracie Fields and politician Cyril Smith. From 1991 to 1996, Wayne attended Springhill High School in the town, close to the M62 motorway. He had an enjoyable time at school especially as playing rugby league was a big part of his life.

Later the same month Wayne was born; Swinton played Rochdale Hornets at Station Road in the Second Division. The Lions won by 24 points to 20. This particular fixture is one of the oldest in Lancashire of any code of football. The Swinton club have played Rochdale Hornets continuously since 1871 which is the year the Rugby Football Union was formed. So, it is fitting that someone born in Rochdale who went on to play for Swinton with such distinction should arrive into the world at the same time these two local rivals were battling it out in a league game. The two teams have continued to battle it out on the pitch and since 2000 the Lions have benefited hugely from having a player at full-back with Rochdale connections. This is reminiscent of when Kenny Gowers wore the famous blue and white of Swinton for 19 seasons from 1954 to 1973 since his father, Walter Gowers, was a stalwart for Rochdale Hornets in the 1920s.

Growing-up in the late 1980s and early 1990s and playing rugby league, Wayne was influenced inevitably by the great Wigan side of that era. In particular, two Wigan players were childhood heroes for Wayne, but they had different routes to the top of the game. One was born in Hackney, north London and played rugby union for Rosslyn Park before Doug Laughton signed him for Widnes in 1987. He went on to become one of the all-time top try scorers in Rugby League, a television personality and a household name. The other was born in Hunslet, south Leeds and played rugby league for Wigan before signing eventually for Sales Sharks in rugby union. He went on to win the Rugby Union World Cup with England in 2003 after a glittering league career with Wigan and Great Britain, which also made him a household name. Both players made a similar journey to the very pinnacle of world rugby albeit in the opposite direction. The first player is Martin Offiah and the second player is Jason Robinson. It is significant that Wayne's favourite players from his childhood were two individuals with the most attacking flair in the game at the time. Although both players tended to play on the wing (in both rugby league and rugby union) Offiah had the sheer pace to beat the best and Robinson had the raw power to do the same. In addition, Robinson had the tactical awareness to play full-back which proved inspirational to Wayne while he was learning the game. In effect, Robinson used his attacking guile at full-back as the best form of defence, which is always a good lesson for any up and coming young player.

The call of rugby league
Wayne does not look like the stereo-typical rugby league player. He is not tall or big and in fact resembles a soccer player in appearance. So, the reason why he chose to play rugby rather than association football is an interesting one not least since the town of Rochdale boasts both codes of professional football; association and rugby league. The truth is simply that Wayne actually enjoys the physical, combative nature of rugby league more than association football. Tackling and being tackled in rugby league takes courage and strength and Wayne has more than adapted to these rigorous activities in spite of his relatively small stature. In addition, Wayne is also very quick and athletic which he uses to his advantage on a rugby pitch. These attributes are something many bigger and bulkier players are unable to cope with, especially when the game is played at such high speed. Moreover, many of Wayne's school friends played the oval ball game and so it was a natural choice for him to play rugby league. In particular, his close friend Tony Appleyard was a big influence on Wayne at a young age. Wayne has remained good friends with many of his former team-mates wherever he has played.

Wayne was about nine years old when he first started playing rugby league. He began playing for one of the many local amateur clubs in the Rochdale area because his primary school did not have a team. This situation is common for many young sports people, where schools have insufficient time or limited resources to nurture sporting talent. As a consequence, during his schooldays Wayne played for several local amateur rugby league teams and eventually was selected for the Rochdale town team. Being selected to play for the town was a great honour for Wayne who valued the representative structure of the amateur game at the school-age level. This gave him the confidence that any young player starting a career needs and it encouraged him to continue with the hard graft of training on a regular basis.

In April 1990, Wayne, along with team-mates from his junior rugby league club from Rochdale, attended the Challenge Cup Final between Wigan and Warrington at the old Wembley Stadium. It was a truly epic encounter between the all-conquering Wigan team captained by the peerless Ellery Hanley and the rapidly developing Warrington team captained by the inspirational Mike Gregory. The clash between two outstanding sides was a glorious affair with the score locked 16–8 in favour of Wigan at half-time before they took control and won 36–14. The two opposing loose-forwards, Hanley and Gregory, battled for supremacy throughout as the 77,729 spectators were superbly entertained. The game and the occasion made a lasting impression on the young Wayne English who would be given his professional debut a decade later when Mike Gregory became Swinton coach. Wayne would encounter Ellery Hanley too, when playing against St Helens and Doncaster coached by Ellery after his wonderful playing career had ended.

One of the very first people to recognise Wayne's talent as a rugby player was Brent Andrews, who coached him in the Rochdale town team under-11 age group. Brent is also from Rochdale and has a fine sporting background of his own. His father played professional football for Rochdale and Bury while Brent played professional rugby league, first for Mansfield Marksmen and then for Nottingham City. In total, he played 54 times, scoring four tries in a career from 1989 to 1991, and featured in most positions in the backs and occasionally in the pack. Brent witnessed plenty of raw talent in the young Wayne English as well as "a willingness to take on everyone." He remembers Wayne being full of enthusiasm for the game typified by a "first at training" attitude even from an early age. It was apparent that Wayne would run all day making breaks and tackling although he did not want to pass the ball too often. However, he soon learned the value of being a team player. Given Brent's own experience, he knew Wayne had all the right attributes to be successful. However, at this stage, Wayne had not settled exclusively into the full-back position and would also play at stand-off from time-to-time. The highlight of this time was the town team playing a game as a curtain-raiser at Thrum Hall, Halifax and a jaunt to play a game at Newcastle-under-Lyme, Staffordshire during which Brent had the dubious honour of driving the team mini-bus. Wayne had got the best possible starts under the guidance of a coach with good experience and a sound knowledge of the game.

It was around this time as well that Wayne attended a Swinton versus Rochdale Hornets game at Station Road. He went with his father and a family friend who happened to support the Lions. As Wayne entered the great arena to watch his home town team, little did he realise at the time that one day he would become a loyal stalwart of their fierce Lancashire rivals.

In time, Wayne was selected to represent Lancashire schoolboys at county level. Wayne played several times for the county team and he still regards this as a great honour. Being selected for the county as a schoolboy is another sign from external sources that progress is being made by any aspiring player. In the same Lancashire squad were players such as Neil Turley and Dwayne West, both of whom went on to make an impact at the professional level. Neil Turley is the son of former Blackpool, Leigh, Swinton and Rochdale Hornets player, Norman Turley. In time, Neil became the mainstay of the Leigh club and was instrumental in the club being promoted into Super League in 2005. However, injury prevented Neil from playing more than a handful of games for Leigh in Super League in which he scored two tries and 20 goals. Dwayne West also played in Super League first for Wigan in the 1999 season and then for St Helens between 2000 and 2002 making eight appearances plus 16 as substitute and in the process scored six tries for the Saints. Wayne also had a career ahead of him in the professional ranks. However, first he had to prove himself as a top amateur player, which he did at Kirkholt WMC.

Kirkholt WMC
Kirkholt is part of the Metropolitan Borough of Rochdale and is located to the south of the Rochdale town centre. It is an area in effect defined where two motorways meet, the M62 to the south and the A627M to the west. Kirkholt is actually where the A627M which connects Oldham and Rochdale crosses the trans-Pennine M62 at junction 20. The A664 Queensway to the north and A671 Oldham Road to the east are the other main routes through Kirkholt. Kirkholt is one of the largest housing estates in the country with 9,000 residents across 300 acres. It was built originally by German prisoners of war in 1945 and due to its size is self-contained with many shops, schools and a community centre. One claim to fame for the area is that Andy Morris is from Kirkholt who was a member of a pop band called Blue Zone along with a local Rochdale singer named Lisa Stansfield.

Since Kirkholt is so close to the M62 motorway and in view of the Pennine hills, it is right at the heart of rugby league country. Therefore, it is only natural that the athletics section of the Kirkholt Working Men's Club (WMC) play rugby league and have done so for many years. The club president for a long time was Peter Standring, a former well known amateur player in his day. The club's headquarters are located in the Kirkholt WMC which is situated on the Strand in a central part of Kirkholt. The team is nicknamed the 'Club', train at Hill Top School and play at Balderstone Community School since both are in the Kirkholt area. The team originally played in the Pennine League for many seasons, but opted for the North West Counties League in the mid-1990s, which involves playing teams from across Lancashire and Cumbria. The Club had decided previously against playing in the North West Counties because there was more travelling involved usually against tougher opposition. They had remained for many years in the Pennine League, playing fixtures with local teams which fitted in with the work and shift patterns of the players. Nevertheless, in their debut season in the North West Counties League, Kirkholt acquitted themselves well lead ably on the field by Tony Appleyard and Darren Brown. Playing at full-back was a young Wayne English who together with many other players had worked their way through the junior ranks of the club into the first team.

Wayne played for Kirkholt in the open age section while still a teenager. Playing in the North West Counties Division Four, Kirkholt had to battle hard against some difficult opponents in the mid-1990s. Local rivalry with Mayfield 'A' provided extra incentive for the team to perform well. In the home game against Mayfield 'A' Wayne was given the man-of-the-match award for a superb tally of four tries as Kirkholt won 64–4. One incident in that match saw Wayne gather the ball from a Mayfield kick; he then slipped between two defenders and rounded the full-back for a fine individual try. The following week, Kirkholt travelled to Cumbria to face Lowca in the BARLA National Cup. Although the team lost 42-24 there was another fine try by Wayne English. He chipped the ball over the defence and plucked the ball from the grasp of the Lowca full-back before crossing for a try which he converted himself. Solid team performances saw Wayne scoring many more tries and goals even winning the man-of-the-match award against Trafford SMOB and UGB from St Helens. Also, Kirkholt did the double over their neighbours from Castleton winning 35–2 away after an outstanding team performance.

Wayne was developing his distinctive style of attacking rugby. In a 42–24 win at Leigh Harriers, Wayne once again chipped over the opposing defence and gathered the ball to score at a crucial stage of the game. In an even tighter 26–21 win at Weaverham, Wayne gathered a loose ball leaving three defenders grasping at his collar to sprint 75 metres for a try, which again he converted himself. There were also set-backs including defeat at the hands of Wigan Tech and Saddleworth, but promotion to Division Three was finally achieved at Preston over Bamber Bridge. A 58–12 victory witnessed another hat-trick and man-of-the-match performance by Wayne although there was a broken leg for team-mate Scott Wilson during the game. Notwithstanding, given such star performances albeit in a good developing team, it became inevitable that Wayne would draw the attention of the local professional clubs including Rochdale Hornets, Oldham and Swinton.

Wayne's final appearance for Kirkholt was in the Joe Kershaw memorial seven-a-side tournament at Keswick Street, Mayfield in 1998. In the first round Kirkholt beat Oldham St Annes 16–10 and then beat Industry, a works team, 34–0 in the next round. The semi-final saw Kirkholt play newly-formed Royton Tigers who were tipped as competition favourites. The team stuck to their task well and won eventually 20–6 and so set-up a final against local rivals Mayfield. In an earlier round, Mayfield had beaten a Joe Kershaw Select which had contained former Featherstone Rovers, Salford and Great Britain star, Steve Nash. A Kirkholt versus Mayfield encounter was a repeat of the final in the previous year, won by Mayfield. Chris Butterworth gave Kirkholt the lead before Mayfield replied through Wayne Hartley. A further three tries for Kirkholt allowed them to take control and a touchline conversion from Wayne English helped to seal a 32–16 victory. Wayne was made captain for the day and given a perfect send-off by his team-mates as it was revealed that he had recently signed a four-year professional contract with Swinton Lions. In typically modest fashion, Wayne remained very grateful to those at Kirkholt who had helped him in the amateur game.

One person in particular who Wayne was grateful towards was John Prince, the Swinton development manager at the time. John was to become something of a mentor to Wayne as he left the amateur ranks for a professional club. John had persuaded Wayne and his father Mike that Swinton offered the most realistic chance of first-team rugby. As it turned out this statement was completely true and indicative of the sincere way that John Prince dealt with the young players. John had played professional rugby league for Leigh and Huyton in the 1970s and even featured in the same Huyton team as former Swinton great Don Preston, whose grandfather Jack Preston had played in the Lions side who beat Salford in the 1900 Challenge Cup Final.

John had played at a time when the game was very physical, certainly knew his way around the rugby field and also how to look after himself. It is this inner-belief and self-confidence that any young player appreciates and aspires towards. There is no doubt that John Prince was a very positive influence on Wayne English when he arrived at Swinton. From this solid start, Wayne was able to begin his professional career in earnest, but he knew that a great deal of hard work and training was needed before he could attempt to break into the first-team.

Heading for glory: Wayne English celebrates with his Kirkholt team-mates after winning the Joe Kershaw seven-a-side rugby league tournament at Mayfield in the summer of 1998.
(Courtesy *Rochdale Observer*)

Signing for Swinton

The 19th (and last) edition of the *Rothman's Rugby League Yearbook* records duly Wayne's entry into world of professional rugby league. On page 112 under the heading "Swinton 1998 signings register" it notes that Wayne English signed on 22 July 1998 from Kirkholt WMC. With this signing Wayne became the first Swinton player to be born in the 1980s. He also signed that season along with former Super League players such as Paul Hulme, George Mann and Ian Watson, who was once a Swinton ball-boy in the days at Station Road.

In the *Rochdale Observer* it was noted: "Rising star Wayne English has signed a four-year contract with Swinton Lions. The 17-year old Kirkholt player impressed Swinton's coaching staff with a series of excellent performances in the Academy team. Wayne, who can play either full-back or half-back, said he wanted to thank the people who have helped develop his career. 'I owe a lot of people like Martin and Val Pickering, Mick Wild, Binnie Connolly and Jimmy Brennan and everyone who has assisted me with my coaching over the last 10 years. I am also indebted to everyone who's sponsored me over the years.'"

Wayne signed for Swinton when the club was based at Gigg Lane, Bury. Six years earlier the club had sold its spiritual home of Station Road for development and moved from the area of Swinton and Pendlebury to Bury. It was a bold move designed to remove the club from debt and make a new start in partnership with a professional football club. In the years immediately following the move the entire complex at Gigg Lane underwent renovation, including rebuilding stands in the stadium, installing a gym and training area for the players and building all-weather pitches on the car park. Bury even played in the same blue and white colours as Swinton, but the ground was not in the Borough of Swinton and Pendlebury and consequently many Swinton fans resented this situation. Nevertheless, Wayne joined the club with Malcolm White as chairman and Tony Barrow as chief executive. Also, there was a good squad of players and a sense of purpose about the club.

Loyalty is a scarce commodity in modern professional sport, even in rugby league where teamwork is paramount. As a Rochdale lad, Wayne has no actual connection to the Swinton area at any level. He was not born in Swinton and has never lived in the town. So, as he began a career in the professional game, Wayne must have considered the future and what the highs and lows were ahead of him. Whatever he contemplated at this stage it is unlikely that he would have imagined that in rugby league circles he would become synonymous with Swinton.

Every step in a journey can present challenges and when Wayne signed for Swinton he was facing his most difficult task to date. Although the Lions were not a Super League outfit, they had in their ranks players who had Super League experience and others who would go on to gain Super League experience. It is inevitable that Wayne was taken aback initially at the size of some of the Swinton players. He knew he had to work extra hard to make an impact and was up for the challenge. He also knew that once he was given a chance in the first-team he had to prove to himself to others that he was good enough to wear the Swinton shirt. Wayne had a suitable tutor on his side in John Prince. The Swinton development manager took him under his wing and taught him how to conduct himself as a professional both on-and-off the field of play. Wayne did not want to let anyone down; not himself, his family, his friends at Kirkholt or his new team-mates Swinton and their loyal band of supporters. In the *Rochdale Observer* at the time Wayne was quoted as saying: "I hope I can repay people's kindness and faith in me, at Swinton." He wasn't to know it in 1998, but this determination to succeed would carry him forward over the next 10 years.

2. The first five years: 1999 to 2003

"The money I got brought in the likes of Ian Pickavance, Jon Neill and Phil Veivers – older, wiser more experienced players. These were to complement a relatively young team, with players like Wayne English, Shaun Fury and Mick Nanyn."
Mike Gregory (2006) writing about his experience as Swinton coach

Introduction

Wayne English arrived at Swinton when the club was based at Gigg Lane, the long-time home of Bury Football Club. Swinton moved to Bury in the summer of 1992 after serious financial problems apparently forced the club to sell Station Road its former ground and spiritual home. Generations of spectators before had witnessed Swinton winning Rugby League Championships and Station Road had also been selected as a primary venue for International test matches, Championship finals, Challenge Cup semi-finals and Lancashire Cup Finals. The glory days on the pitch for the Swinton club came to an end in the early 1970s and the last major trophy the Lions won was victory over Leigh in the Lancashire Cup Final in the 1969–70 season. A reduced spectator base meant that the upkeep of the vast Station Road ground was becoming more and more difficult especially once major showpiece rugby league games ceased being played at the venue after the 1984 Challenge Cup semi-final between Widnes and Leeds attended by 14,046 spectators.

The first five years of Wayne's time at Swinton had its own share of financial problems as many Swinton fans drifted away, still refusing to go to Bury for home games, some six miles across north Manchester. When the Lions moved initially, in spite of its homely appeal, the Gigg Lane ground was in need of a major up-grade. The decision by the football club at Bury to ground-share with the Lions meant that money was found eventually to up-grade facilities from sources such as the National Lottery and the Football Foundation. Consequently, throughout the 1990s, Gigg Lane was home to Swinton RLFC as well as Bury FC as the sign on the car park wall proclaimed proudly.

1999: Academy days

Having signed for the Lions in the summer of 1998, Wayne had to wait a further 18 months before making his first team debut. The delay was due in part to a serious cruciate ligament injury. Fortunately for him, Swinton had a very good academy set-up at the time and so the year of recovery was not wasted totally. As it happened, this was also good planning on behalf of the club. Without this academy set-up, Swinton may have missed the opportunity to discover and then nurture one its most gifted players since leaving Station Road. A great deal of the credit for Wayne's early development has to go to John Prince as well as Les

Holliday, who was Swinton coach when Wayne signed. Les Holliday is a Swinton legend and one of the very few players to merit this title since the halcyon days of Gowers, Buckley, Stopford and Blan in the 1960s. Les made his Swinton debut on 14 December 1982 at home to Doncaster and his final game was at Rochdale Hornets on 27 July 1997 having played for Halifax, Widnes and Dewsbury in between as well as representing Great Britain and playing at Wembley for Halifax. Over the years, Swinton, including Wayne, have benefited enormously from Les Holliday at the club as player, coach and director of rugby as well as a stalwart of the club's tradition and heritage. Of course, some Swinton fans would argue that since the 1960s Danny Wilson is worthy of the legend status as well. Wilson was masterful at his best in the 1980s and as the father of Manchester United footballer Ryan Giggs he has certainly given the Swinton club considerable fame albeit through reflected glory. As for Wayne English, he was happy to sign for the club and watch the first-team when he could.

With Wayne in the Academy and recovering from injury, the 1999 season started for the first-team in January with a comfortable win at home to amateur side Moldgreen from Huddersfield in the third round of the Challenge Cup. Long-serving winger Simon Ashcroft scored a hat-tick and the Lions were marshalled well by local player Ian Watson in the half-backs. The Northern Ford Premiership (NFP) had been unveiled earlier in the month and the non-Super League teams formed a single effective division. However, given there were 18 clubs it was decided that every team would not play one another on a home-and-away basis; rather there would be a total of 28 games and a top-five play-off series at the end of the season. The first league game in February was at home to Hunslet and the visitors won 21–10 in spite of a creditable performance by in-form full-back Mark Welsby.

The fourth round of the Challenge Cup pitted the Lions against Super League opposition. The trip to the impressive McAlpine Stadium to play the Huddersfield Giants was always going to be a tough encounter for the Lions. As it transpired, the Giants hit the Lions hard and soon raced into an early lead, winning eventually 78–4. Three tries from Craig Weston and two tries each for Paul Cook and Danny Arnold plus 10 goals from Bobbie Goulding caused the damage to the luckless Lions. A late Ryan Stazicker try was the only consolation for the travelling Swinton supporters as the team avoided narrowly the ignominy of the all-time worst defeat for the Lions.

Back to the league, and another trip to Yorkshire also proved fruitless for the Lions. This time a visit to Doncaster where a narrow 22–18 defeat was not a good return given that Doncaster, then known as the Dragons and in a state of transition, eventually finished bottom of the table in spite of signing former Great Britain international Garry Schofield for a period.

The league season finally got into winning ways with a home victory over Bramley in which tries from Damien Cleary, Cliff Eccles and Carl McCabe provided the platform. A close game at York followed where the Lions lost by a single point in spite of an early lead through a Marlon Billy try. He had recently signed from Keighley and his brother Chris coincidentally played at Gigg Lane for Bury FC. In March, the Lions signed another winger, Richard Henare, who had Super League experience with Warrington scoring 24 tries in 28 appearances between 1996 and 1997. Richard scored his first Swinton try in the 29–19 defeat at home to Dewsbury.

To underline his worth to the team, Ian Watson inspired the Lions to victory at Whitehaven in the next match, scoring a try and kicking two goals in a rare 12–4 victory at the Recreation Ground. To follow up this fine result, the Lions beat Rochdale Hornets at home, albeit by four points, and Australian Gavin Price-Jones scored to set the team on its way. Around April, Mike Gregory, the former Warrington and Great Britain second- row forward joined the Lions coaching staff, having been persuaded to join the club by chairman Malcolm White. Gregory had been coaching previously at St Helens under head coach Shaun McRae.

Four defeats followed on the bounce. The defeat at Featherstone was expected and Barrow sent a competitive team to Gigg Lane in the next game. Widnes away and Leigh at home were tough encounters in which the Lions played gritty rugby league, but never looked like winning in spite of solid displays from the likes of Mark Welsby at full-back, Ian Watson at half-back and Sean Casey in the back-row. Les Holliday resigned at this point after finding it difficult to combine coaching with work commitments.

In May, Mike Gregory was installed as head coach at Swinton. In his autobiography, *Biting back* published in 2006, Gregory reveals he had a good working relationship with chief executive Tony Barrow because he was left to do the coaching. The coaching job at Swinton was part-time although Gregory received a car and the use of a telephone. He was supported by the talented John Prince in the role of development manager, Norman Brown as physiotherapist and Eric Skeetch as kit-man. Gregory lamented there was no-one in the role of conditioner as this took him away from a purely coaching capacity. So he acted quickly to appoint former Warrington conditioner Les Chadwick in this position on a part-time basis.

The next phase of the season witnessed an improvement in the fortunes of the club on the playing side as the Academy team were improving, too with Wayne still recovering from injury. A fine victory against Lancashire Lynx at Victory Park, Chorley was most welcome, not least because of another two tries and an outstanding display from Sean Casey, a player who had competed with Keiron Cunningham for the number nine shirt at St Helens at the start of his career. Another narrow defeat by a single point at home to Keighley was followed by a win over Oldham, a club still in the process of regrouping under chairman Chris Hamilton after the collapse of the former club and exit from Super League in 1997.

Three tough away trips in June to Workington Town, Hull KR and Hunslet all ended in defeat, in spite of some valiant efforts at such formidable grounds. Paul Smith emerged with credit from these games as did the reliable Sean Casey, Steve Gartland, Ian Watson and Mark Welsby. It was no consolation to the Swinton supporters but at least the grass at Gigg Lane had been given the opportunity to flourish while the Lions were touring the north of England in search of league points.

Also in June, it was reported that Malcolm White was proposing a merger between Swinton and arch-rivals and near-neighbours Salford. There was much speculation at the time that talks were more advanced than many people realised and the prospect of a combined Manchester Rugby League Football Club was more than a pipe dream. In the fullness of time, nothing ever materialised although arguments over where to play, the colour of any playing kit and of course the new nickname would have raged for a long time assuming both sets of supporters would have accepted the deal, which was not very likely in any event. Nevertheless, the future of Swinton Lions did seem very precarious at this time.

Doncaster were next up at Gigg Lane and the Lions won convincingly 48–2, including a superb hat-tick from Mark Welsby and a great display from former Widnes stalwart Richie Eyres. A 20–14 loss at Bramley was one of the strangest experiences of the season. A paltry total of 354 fans witnessed the game at the huge Headingley complex in Leeds, where Bramley had been playing since 1997. It was clear to everyone at the game that life outside Super League would be tough going for clubs such as Bramley and Swinton. Indeed, after 103 years of history, Bramley finished as a professional club at the end of the season.

Two home victories by similar margins against Batley and York revived hopes of a spirited end of season run in. However, the third loss of the season by a single point this time at Dewsbury ensured a mid-table finish was the most likely outcome. Incidentally, the Lions lost three other games by two or three points during the course of the season in spite of Ian Watson scoring seven drop-goals. The Lions did bounce back with a 51–28 win at home to Whitehaven where a Richard Henare hat-trick was the star-billing.

The season finished disappointingly with one win from the final five games including three more narrow defeats. The win occurred at Barrow where two Ian Watson tries complemented two tries in the debut season of Mick Nanyn who signalled his impressive arrival in professional rugby league. The final game of the season ended with a 22–20 defeat at Leigh and confirmed the Lions in 13th spot after a 28 game season. Swinton were far short of the top five league position that they achieved in the previous season as Hunslet and Dewsbury contested the NFP Grand Final at Headingley.

Towards the end of the season on 11 August, John Prince suffered serious injury following an awful accident in which he fell down a full flight of stairs at home. He broke his neck in two places as well as endured other broken bones. After a prolonged period of hospitalisation the full extent of John's injuries became apparent, but the enduring result was that the club could no longer call upon the invaluable services of an exceptional person. Mike Gregory described John Prince as "a very gifted person" who did a great deal of excellent work coaching and promoting the game to schools. In addition, he was dealing with players in the amateur game and the younger players at the club such as Wayne English.

Of course, no-one knows what John Prince could have achieved with Swinton and speculating is sometimes unhelpful. Notwithstanding, there are many people connected to the club such as former director Richard Taylor who believe that John Prince had all the right qualities to be a future Swinton coach. Even though journalist and author Dave Hadfield in his acclaimed book "*Up and over: a trek through rugby league land*" declares that the position of the head coach at the Lions is a tough task. To quote, it is like "being a good father" as it is "one of those impossible jobs, like managing Leeds United, coaching Swinton or leading the Conservative Party." Nevertheless, John had the right blend of playing experience at the professional level for Leigh and Huyton as well as an outstanding coaching ability at any level. John Prince can read rugby league games very well indeed and assess the attributes of players. Whenever Mike Gregory mentioned the name of a player, John Prince knew everything there was to know about him. As John Prince embarked on his long journey of rehabilitation, the officials at Swinton were left to reflect on what might have been. Moreover, Wayne had also suffered a serious knee injury that required nearly a year of rehabilitation which delayed his first-team debut, but was now on the road to recovery.

2000: First team debut

Wayne made his full Swinton debut just a few weeks after the start of a new millennium. Having been signed by one former Great Britain forward, Les Holliday, he was given his break into the first-team by another, Mike Gregory, who was at the helm the night Wayne burst into the Swinton team. In his autobiography, Mike Gregory reflected that he brought in some experienced players at the time including former St Helens trio Ian Pickavance, Jon Neill and Phil Veivers to complement a relatively young team with players like Wayne English, Shaun Furey and Mick Nanyn. Also in his book, Mike was generous with his praise for John Prince who was an influential figure at the club and partially responsible for bringing Wayne to Swinton in the first place.

The 2000 NFP season started with a set of mixed results for the Lions. A rare victory at Workington Town's notoriously daunting Derwent Park on Boxing Day 1999 meant the season started in fine form. The day after the dawn of the new millennium, the Lions hosted Oldham and there was a fantastic crowd of 2,567 at Gigg Lane. As the supporters snaked their way around the vast car park in front of the main stand queuing to gain entrance to the game, it was reminiscent of the good old days when the demand to watch a Swinton versus Oldham match at this time of the year was always high. Oldham won a keenly found contest 23–18. Another rare away victory in the next game, at Leigh's Hilton Park by two points, saw Swinton's prospects improve again. This was followed by a comfortable win over Lancashire Lynx. Another narrow defeat at Widnes followed with the Lions at least competing with the best in the league.

On the 1 February 2000, Wayne English made his first-team debut for the Lions in the third round Challenge Cup against Waterhead, an amateur team from Oldham. The Lions won comfortably 74–1 in the end, including tries from Tony Barrow junior, Sean Casey, Andy Craig and Andy Coley with the biggest cheer of the match reserved for the Waterhead drop-goal. Wayne made his mark on the game by making a try-scoring debut, not just in his first outing for Swinton, but also in his first professional match. Wayne would prove his worth over and over again and certainly he would never let anyone down as he didn't on his debut.

The fourth round of the Challenge Cup matched the Lions at home to St. Helens. One of the biggest ever crowds at Gigg Lane of 3,169 spectators witnessed a fantastic match between these two old Lancashire rivals. There have been many epic contests between the Lions and Saints not least in the 1960s when Johnny Stopford played opposite Tom van Vollenhoven. This game had its fair share of spice as well with several Swinton players formerly at Saints including Sean Casey, Jonathon Neill, Paul Loughlin and Ian Pickavance, albeit that Pickavance started his professional career at Swinton in 1988–89 when the club was still based at Station Road. The Lions held their own for long periods in the game and won many contests all over the pitch, even leading 16-10 at half time. If anything the final score of 36–22 to Saints flattered the Super League side who had been given a good test by the Lions. Saints won due in part to a fine Keiron Cunningham display and a Kevin Iro hat-trick. In his autobiography, Swinton coach Mike Gregory revealed that after the game his Saints counterpart Ellery Hanley in a rare display of openness asked if he could talk to the Swinton players after the game. An emotional Hanley is reported to have said in the Swinton dressing room: "If you play like that and stick together the way you did you'll all be successful." It was a great gesture from a truly great rugby league player. For various reasons, Ellery has been largely misunderstood and even misrepresented in popular opinion outside the game, but there can be little doubt that he was the greatest British rugby league player of his generation, a view supported fully by the respect he earned in Australia. During this period Wayne was being picked regularly in the first-team although he was not selected for the Saints game and watched the game from the touchline.

There was the small matter of the rest of the season to deal with next, even though this was of little comfort to the supporters, it was very important to the club. The players responded well and won narrowly at Whitehaven after a long trek to West Cumbria and followed up the result by beating Barrow at home. Next, defeat at Hull KR was not surprising, but defeat at home to Keighley and a loss at Doncaster were somewhat unexpected, leaving the Lions losing some of the momentum gained from the Saints game. The mini-slump was halted by a thrilling 14–14 draw with Dewsbury. This was followed by two home victories against Sheffield and Workington, including a try in each game for Wayne English, along with other tries for the established first-team players such as Richard Henare, Mick Nanyn, Ian Watson and Jason Roach, recently signed again after three years in Super League.

There then followed another three-match loosing streak including defeats at Oldham and Featherstone - featuring three cousins playing for Swinton namely, Steve, Paul and Tony Barrow - before the final third of the season saw a relatively decent run of form in which only four games were lost in the final 10 matches. The influence of Mike Gregory, who had many contacts in his native

Wigan, created an unusual venue for the Lions to play a home match. The fixture with Whitehaven was played at the Half Edge ground of Orrell Rugby Union Football Club and ended in a 28–28 draw at the small, well-appointed venue that had been used by the Lions as a training base since Christmas. Wayne English travelled to watch the game although did not play. This is the only venue where the Swinton first team has played a home fixture since leaving Station Road that has not featured Wayne English on the teamsheet.

The last three games of the season were up-and-down for the Lions. A defeat at Barrow was followed by a fine win against York scoring 50 points in the process, including tries from Phil Coussons, Jason Roach, Paul Loughlin and Wayne English. The season finished with a poor performance in early July at Keighley where the Lions went down 66–12. A total of 13 wins and two draws was an improvement on the previous NFP season and this was reflected in a higher league placing of ninth. There was no doubt that progress was being made on the field of play, but in addition there was frustration that the rate of improvement was not better.

This season marked the end of the playing career of two outstanding Swinton players both due to injury, loose-forward Sean Casey and full-back Mark Welsby. Sean, signed on 4 December 1996 from Whitehaven, had all the hallmarks of a quality pack-leader and would prove to be a great loss. Mark, signed on 5 June 1992 from Wigan, gave the Lions eight wonderful years of service at Gigg Lane. He was solid in defence and always ready to join the attacking line. Although Wayne was not quite ready to make the number one spot his own, he had made his debut, had gained valuable first team experience and had a great role model in Mark Welsby.

The climax of the 2000 Northern Ford Premiership was the Grand Final between Dewsbury and Leigh played at Gigg Lane on Saturday 29 July. In a thrilling game, the Yorkshire side edged the contest 13–12 after a late drop-goal by Richard Agar. The entire occasion brought back memories for the many Swinton supporters in the crowd of 8,487. Here was the ground of the Swinton club hosting a great rugby league event, well supported with a feel good factor. The problem was that the ground was located in Bury and not Swinton. In any case, the game was staged perfectly at Gigg Lane with the spectators, the majority from Leigh, adding to a tremendous atmosphere before and during the game as the players performed fittingly to a very high standard indeed. For those connected to Swinton too, there was a glimpse of what might have been had senior officials at the club in 1992 decided to remain at Station Road and seek to redevelop the ground rather than sell it for housing and relocate.

2001: Establishing a reputation

With the first-team debut under his belt, the 2001 season dawned bright for Wayne but he still had to train hard and develop his skills in order to gain a regular first-team place. Competition for places is exactly what keeps players on their toes and makes them fight as hard as possible to get selected. Although it is possible to argue that the best Swinton side since leaving Station Road was the team of 1998 in terms of final league position, there were still many talented footballers in the squad to drive Wayne forward and continue to be determined to wear the full-back shirt. Incidentally, the Swinton shirt this season was sponsored by *The Independent* newspaper which was edited by Swinton supporter Simon Kelner.

The 2001 season started with three straight wins in the latter part of the calendar year 2000. The NFP was another 28 game season, containing 18 teams including the Lions. A sound win at Chorley in early December set the tone with Mick Nanyn in great form scoring two tries and three goals. A trip to Whitehaven also netted a win in an unusually low-scoring game by 8–4. Mike Gregory was particularly pleased with this result as he got one over on his former Warrington team-mate Paul Cullen. A two point win at Gigg Lane over Barrow catapulted the Lions into third place in the league. However, the mirror image of the result occurred in the next three games as a heavy defeat at Leigh was followed by an 8–4 defeat at home to Rochdale and narrow defeat at Widnes. One pleasing aspect was that the Lions defence was improving as expected under the coaching of Mike Gregory.

The third round of the Challenge Cup paired the Lions with the New Earswick All Blacks, an amateur side from the York area. Swinton won 44–12, the highlight of which was a try from former Salford player Carlo Napolitano. A home loss to Workington Town followed, in spite of some good play from former St Helens star and inspirational player Phil Veivers, who had recently joined and was using his experience to improve the younger players.

The next Swinton game proved infamous for everyone concerned with the club. Leeds in the fourth round of the Challenge Cup should have been a showcase for the talents of the Swinton players and the ability of Gigg Lane to stage major games of rugby league. As it happened, Leeds showed no mercy whatsoever; nor should they have, of course. The Lions started brightly and Paul Loughlin even scored a well-worked try in front of 3,239 spectators. However, Leeds had a very talented squad coached by Dean Bell. Brett Mullins, Bradley Clyde, Iestyn Harris, Keith Senior, Adrian Morley, Barrie McDermott and Kevin Sinfield all played for Leeds that afternoon as the Lions were hammered 106–10 in a clinical and ruthless display of modern rugby league. This result was the worst defeat for Swinton in the history of the club. Interestingly, Mike Gregory never watched the video of the game afterwards which he regarded as the lowest point in his coaching career. On reflection, the game could be seen as a parable for the game in the Super League era, where the rich get richer and the modern methods of coaching and conditioning mean part-time players can not hope to compete meaningfully with full-time professionals. Malcolm White persuaded Mike Gregory to remain as Swinton coach and to his credit Mike remained loyal after what was a truly dreadful experience. He never blamed the players such as Wayne, who all tried their best as he knew that Leeds had played exceptionally well and simply exploited their superiority to maximum effect.

The fall out from the Leeds game continued with three more defeats in the weeks that followed, including losses at Hunslet and Hull KR. Many Swinton supporters were sanguine about playing Hull KR away for the second season in succession without a home fixture in return. It seemed that Rovers could not find Bury on a map, especially when the Lions were always drawn away to Hull KR in cup competitions as well.

A 28–25 home win over Featherstone Rovers in mid-March restored a great deal of confidence in the Swinton players, with John Paul Doherty in particular performing well in the pack and local player Lee Hudson excelling with two tries. In the next game, Swinton beat York 74–0 at Gigg Lane which simply served to prove that the Minstermen had troubles of their own. Mick Nanyn scored three tries and nine goals totalling 30 points which equalled the modern day club record held by Australian Greg Pearce since 1996 in a game against Prescot Panthers. This game proved the Swinton players possessed talent and that Leeds had simply overawed the young Lions.

The Lions lost the next two home games, including another defeat by a single point, this time to Sheffield Eagles. A good win at Keighley was followed by a heavy defeat at home to Leigh and then a win by a single point over Doncaster at home. The next two games also followed a win-loss pattern before a sequence of seven successive defeats completely knocked the team's already shattered confidence. Although six of these seven defeats were away from home in one of the most uneven fixture lists of recent years, there was no escaping that the better teams could beat Swinton and that Swinton could not raise their game to beat teams of similar ability. Hence, the Lions lost by one point at Doncaster, where Andy Cheetham suffered a bad injury, and by two points at Oldham but were beaten 62–0 at home to Widnes. Hooker Rob Barraclough continued to tackle everything that moved, Matt Bateman showed genuine pace in the centres and prop Lee Hansen never took a backward step, but the Lions were locked in 15th spot in the league with little prospect of moving up the table. The final two games did provide a glimmer of hope as Hunslet and Dewsbury, the two NFP Grand Finalists in 1999, were both beaten. The Hunslet game, played at The Willows because Gigg Lane was unavailable was attended by 823 spectators and saw a fine performance and two tries from Mike Woods. However, Salford seemed reluctant to allow Swinton to play permanently at the Willows. The Dewsbury game was a fantastic display by the entire team and gave the supporters some grounds for future optimism. Two tries for Wayne English with other tries from Mike Woods, Phil Veivers, Mick Nanyn, Jim Evans and Danny Butler must have put a smile back on Mike Gregory's face.

At the end of season presentations, Mike Gregory agreed that the season had had its share of mixed fortune but that the spirit shown by the players in the final two games was indicative of the potential within the squad. Gregory promptly went on tour to Australia and New Zealand with the England Academy side. On returning to Swinton, he was informed by Malcolm White: "We're not renewing your contract." Apparently, the club wanted a coach as head coach with more understanding of the amateur game. This decision was not unexpected and accepted by Mike Gregory in good grace. He later coached his home town club Wigan and guided them to the Challenge Cup final in 2004 before a devastating illness caused him to step down from the job. Mike Gregory sadly passed away in November 2007.

The season marked the end of the playing career of several Swinton stalwarts, including Tony Barrow, the son of the former St Helens player and Swinton coach of the same name who signed in February 1992. The younger Tony Barrow had served the club well throughout the Gigg Lane era and was a talented front-row forward having played previously at Oldham and Thatto Heath ARLFC. He was the last playing link to Station Road, having appeared 10 times for the Lions in the 1991–92 season in the old First Division and retired from the game due to work commitments. In total, Tony made 243 Swinton appearances scoring 25 tries.

Matt Bateman, who had had a decent few seasons, eventually drifted back to the amateur ranks and Jim Evans retired from the professional game as well. Jim's claim to fame, apart from his Swinton career, is that his father, Frank Evans is El Ingles, only the third ever British bull-fighter in Spain. In turn, Frank Evans later became a director at Swinton Lions.

In November 2001 it was announced by chief executive Tony Barrow senior that Swinton would face another 12 months in Bury. He commented "We have tried our best to get set up here in Swinton and we want the supporters to know that we haven't given up; we're still trying and we hope the fans can see that." Also, he urged the supporters to remain loyal to the club and continue to watch the team in Bury. Finally, during the close season the club signed a number of new players including Karl Fitzpatrick, an exciting prospect from Widnes Vikings who was an established BARLA international and played either scrum-half or centre. As for Wayne, his rugby league education was continuing apace and he was getting selected regularly in the first team at full-back and as a substitute contributing five tries in total for the season.

2002: Exit from Bury

It is no exaggeration to state that the 2002 season was perhaps the most troubled for Swinton since its formation in 1866. Although the Lions started the season at Gigg Lane, events were to totally conspire against the club. The Lions effectively left Bury in the summer of 2002 almost 10 years to the day following the contentious and ultimately ill-fated move from Station Road. After a few matches of nomadic existence in Leigh and Chorley the club almost folded. The season finished with some relative stability playing in Kersal and the formation of the Supporters' Trust chaired by Steve Wild with John Kidd in place as the club chairman. Nevertheless, the unsustainable nature of the move to Bury had finally caught up with Swinton. The true reasons behind the move to Gigg Lane are explored fully in Steve Wild's complete history of the club published in 1999. All it is necessary to state at this point is that it would have been wonderful to witness Wayne English use his pace and serve on the wide open spaces of Station Road. However, Wayne, like all his contemporaries in the Swinton shirt, was born too late to play for the Lions there.

The Lions started the campaign in December 2001 with Tony Humphries installed as head coach and Mark Sheals as his assistant. Both were former Swinton players with plenty of rugby league experience at the top level. Craig Dean was handed the captaincy. As before, the RFL continued with the decision to start the NFP season early so that games could be played over the Christmas and New Year period. As it happened, Swinton only played twice, a creditable defeat at home to Hull KR and a disappointing loss away to Rochdale Hornets. This relative inactivity early in the campaign was due to the postponement of several matches. First, there was no safety certificate available in time from Tameside Council for Oldham's ground-share at Hurst Cross (home of Ashton United FC) in the opening game, so the game had to be rescheduled; second there was poor weather over Christmas and New Year. The start of a new calendar year did not bode well for the club either. A defeat at Chorley and then a heavy loss at home to Workington Town saw the Lions enter the Challenge Cup without a win. The Lions were drawn at home in the third round to the top amateur club Skirlaugh from Humberside. The match was postponed on the original date due to further bad weather which meant the relatively large travelling support did not materialise for the rearranged match on the following Wednesday evening. Many of the 206 supporters who attended the game still remember the occasion vividly as Skirlaugh forced extra-time after being in front 14–12 at half-time. Lee Hansen won the man-of-the-match award for Swinton as the Lions eventually won 32–24.

This Challenge Cup victory over with Skirlaugh did not create a platform for either the next round or the following matches in the league. In the fourth round, the Lions were drawn at home to Widnes and this time a large away support arrived for this game much to the benefit of the club's finances. The attendance was 1,638 for the match, which Widnes won convincingly 54–0 after a closer first half ended 18–0 to the visitors. Swinton lost the next five league games including heavy defeats at Dewsbury and Featherstone. While Featherstone's Post Office Road has never been a successful venue for the Lions over the previous four decades, the 75–12 mauling at Dewsbury was a poor performance by any standard.

At this time, Malcolm White resigned as chairman after he had been threatening to do so for a while. To his credit, Tony Barrow took over and rallied the entire club by urging a thousand fans to attend home games. As it happened, in 2002 the club averaged 547 spectators for league games down from 944 in the previous season. The crisis was deepening at the club and it became apparent that a move away from Gigg Lane was imminent now that Malcolm White had stepped down. The only bright note was that Steve Wild was helping to form a Supporters' Trust along with many other loyal fans. The Trust would ultimately help the club secure a long term future following an initial meeting at the historic White Lion pub in Swinton where the team acquired its nickname in 1873. Former Swinton great Alan Buckley was installed as the honorary president of the Supporters' Trust.

Of course, things could always be worse and for York Wasps, a club with a long and proud tradition in the game, it did get worse. York's game at Workington on 17 March 2002 was the club's last and they withdrew from the Rugby Football League with immediate effect part-way through the season. York, like Swinton, was formed as a rugby union club in the 1860s and had a wonderful tradition over many generations, and had also lost their traditional home in the city centre. Clearly, these were difficult times for all clubs especially those outside Super League and York's problems had surfaced the previous season. While the people at York used the remainder of 2002 to regroup and return successfully again in 2003 reincarnated as York City Knights, the Lions had to continue to struggle and things got worse on and off the pitch.

Coach Tony Humphries finally won a game against professional opposition with a spirited 33–6 victory over Keighley at Gigg Lane. This league encounter was a personal triumph for Rob Russell who scored a try and three goals. In the end, this result was insufficient to save Tony his job and he parted company with the club soon afterwards. Tony Barrow senior took over as coach on a temporary basis and Mark Sheals remained as the assistant coach. Interestingly, before he became a professional rugby league player Mark played association football as a junior at Deans Pursuit JFC in Swinton, the club that eventually nurtured Ryan Giggs. The National Cup group games followed with Swinton in the Western Division. There were heavy defeats at Leigh, Barrow and Workington, separated by a narrow loss at home to Chorley on 14 April 2002. The latter game was to be the last ever Swinton game at Gigg Lane almost exactly 10 years after the sale of Station Road was announced. Writing in 1999, Steve Wild expressed grave doubts about the long-term future and viability of Swinton in Bury. In time, he was proved correct as the Lions vacated Gigg Lane ultimately for good but with no permanent ground to fulfil fixtures.

Bury FC has had its own fair share of problems and the revelation that benefactor Hugh Eaves (who even had significant financial connections with Swinton) was not the long-term saviour of the club delivered some home truths for all concerned as he was under investigation for serious financial irregularities. The supporter base at Bury FC was insufficient, (at a level similar to Swinton a decade previously) and change was in the offing. An obvious target for resentment appeared to be Swinton and it was claimed the Lions had paid a peppercorn rent for too long and worst of all allegedly ruined the pitch at Gigg Lane, once regarded as the best playing surface in the Football League. As it happened, the Lions had brought significant benefits to Bury FC including the ability to bid for stadium grants as a multi-use complex and a greater sporting profile such as hosting the Northern Ford Premiership Final between Leigh and Dewsbury in 2000 in front of a capacity crowd. As for the pitch, the Lions had always complied with requests to play a series of away games in the summer months to allow the grass to grow in time for the football season, often to the detriment of results.

Obviously, the Swinton contribution was no longer sufficient or valued and the Lions were forced out of Gigg Lane during the annual period when the Lions were due to play matches away from whilst the pitch was being reseeded. There is no doubt that both parties were ready for a change. Bury FC could use the Gigg Lane Stadium for other purposes such as Manchester United reserves matches, and later FC United of Manchester, and Swinton could move away from Bury which had become such a symbol of simmering discontent for so many disillusioned and stay away fans. However, timing in life is everything and without a permanent ground in place now was not really the time to leave Bury, at least not for the time being. A possible choice of venue for the club could have been a move to The Willows, a couple of miles from the Borough of Swinton and Pendlebury. Swinton had played matches here during World War Two when Station Road had been requisitioned for the war effort. The Lions had played a home fixture at the Willows against Hunslet the previous season when Gigg Lane was temporarily unavailable. The Willows seemed a good choice at least until a permanent ground could be secured for the longer term.

However, a move to the home of the Lions' ach-rivals was not to be as Salford and Swinton were unable or unwilling to agree terms and conditions. This left the Lions without a home with over half the season remaining. By now, it was not beyond the realms of possibility that the 2002 season could have witnessed the end of the Lions part way through the season. In times of need though, true friends pull through and first Leigh and then Chorley allowed Swinton to use Hilton Park and Victory Park, respectively. The Swinton supporters attending these matches will never forget the generosity and kindness showed by Leigh and Chorley in the Lions' darkest hour of need. It is this sort of camaraderie that has shaped Rugby League for over 100 years.

On reflection, a move to The Willows could have created as many problems as it was intended to solve. The Swinton-Salford rivalry is one the oldest in any type of team sport and at times resembles a long-standing bitter feud. For example, as early as the 1884–85 season Swinton had to cancel fixtures between the two clubs following a near riot at the Lions' Stoneacre enclosure caused when an off-the-ball incident had left Swinton player Tom Banks spark out. Even before the game, the legendary Swinton player Jim Valentine had received dire threatening letters, presumably from a Salford source. Indeed, the sporting relationship between the two clubs has been very fierce ever since so when the Lions finally went it alone in early May 2002 it was probably for the best. Around this time, Karl Fitzpatrick left the Lions for Salford under a clause in his contract that allowed NFP players to leave if a Super League club made an offer for them.

The games in exile were not much fun as the Lions looked in imminent danger of collapse in spite of the hard work from Tony Barrow and the other club officials. In spite of a 29–20 win over Whitehaven at Hilton Park, this game effectively brought an end to the Lions' interest in the National Cup as only one win in five had been secured. At this point, former Lions player and Saints' legend Phil Veivers was appointed head coach as the club began to seek more stability. A bizarre event happened in the next home game as Swinton played Leigh at home in Leigh. The away side made the most of home advantage and won 40–6. Three actual away fixtures followed including a memorable win at Whitehaven and defeats at Barrow and Batley. A creditable 24–24 draw against Hunslet at Leigh was followed by a defeat to Barrow at the same venue. A welcome victory at Gateshead was not sustained as heavy defeats at Oldham and Huddersfield followed giving the season a roller-coaster effect. Finally, the Lions were forced to play Featherstone in the league at Victory Park, Chorley and the Yorkshire side won 40–24.

Inevitably, the 10 years at Bury meant a whole generation of folk from Swinton, Pendlebury, Clifton and elsewhere in the surrounding area lost touch with the playing fortunes of the Lions. Many people assumed wrongly that the club no longer existed or that the team had become known as Bury Lions. There is insufficient evidence to know the true nature of the longer term plans that the club had, if the team had remained at Gigg Lane. What is certain is that the experiment had run its course and the fact the proud name of Swinton remained in the professional game of rugby league was a minor miracle (even if the Lions suffix had been added in 1996). Meanwhile around this time, to the south of the City of Manchester, Sale Rugby Union Football Club was also about to become known as Sale Sharks and re-located match-days a few miles away to Edgeley Park, home of Stockport County FC. Sale formed in 1861, acquired the backing of businessman Brian Kennedy and the astute marketing of Peter Deakin, who had achieved outstanding results in rugby league for Warrington Wolves and Bradford Bulls. Therefore, it is conceivable that the original plans of Malcolm White for Swinton could have worked and even been regarded as ahead of its time. Equally, it has to be noted that Sale Sharks play top-flight rugby union and retained the traditional ground in Sale at Heywood Road whilst growing the supporter base in an impressive manner.

Towards the end of the 2002 season, the Lions found some stability with a move to Moor Lane, home of Salford City FC, which is just the other side of the M27 Swinton and Pendlebury postcode across the River Irwell in neighbouring Kersal. On 4 August 2002, the Lions lined-up to play Doncaster with a permanent home in place. On a sunny afternoon, 757 spectators witnessed the first game back in the locality and with hope for a more stable long-term future. 1960s stars Alan Buckley and Ken Gowers were introduced to the players before kick-off. Although the Lions lost 29–12 to a very competitive Doncaster side the result on this occasion did not really matter. The key thing was that the club had been saved and the team was playing close to Swinton.

The Lions played out the rest of the season at Moor Lane with some modest success including three home victories against Chorley, Gateshead and Whitehaven. There were three losses on the road during the same period at Keighley, Sheffield and Leigh. All in all, the Lions finished in 15th place in the Northern Ford Premiership league table showing glimpses of potential which qualified the team for a place in the National League One Play-off series. The Lions played away to Sheffield Eagles in a Friday night fixture at the Don Valley Stadium. In a close game that was contested evenly, the Eagles won 30–20 and so the season ended on the playing front with heads held high after a turbulent period for the club. Tony Barrow summed-up the mood when he wrote in the programme: "[the 2002 season] has without doubt been the hardest I have been through in 41 years in Rugby League."

The players deserve a huge amount of credit during this period for keeping the faith and remaining loyal to the Lions. Club captain Craig Dean was inspirational along side Kiwi Lee Hansen, plus Dale Holdstock and Phil Cushion in the pack, Adrian Mead and Hugh Thorpe on the wings and Mick Nanyn in the centres all of whom played over 20 times during the course of the season with Wayne English contributing some good performances, too. The supporters too never gave up and formed the first ever supporters trust in professional rugby league. Through this organisation the club was able to galvanise cohesive support including Salford City Council. On 4 October Tony Barrow resigned as chief executive allowing John Kidd to be instrumental in helping to save the club and establish a new identity closer to Swinton. By the end of the season neither Malcolm White nor Tony Barrow were at the club and the Bury experiment was at an end as far Swinton Lions RLFC was concerned.

By the end of November Phil Veivers had quit as head coach. The Lions moved quickly to appoint former coach Peter Roe who had enjoyed a previous spell with the club from January 1996 to March 1997 and had successfully led the Lions out of the old Division Two. Earlier in 2002, Roe had been head coach at Wakefield Trinity and also had acted an advisor to Whitehaven underlining his expertise and countless miles travelled in pursuit of employment in rugby league from his home in Keighley. At the time, only Alan Agar and Maurice Bamford had coached at the professional level in all three counties of Cumbria, Lancashire and

Yorkshire. As for the Lions, there was some stability at last on and off the pitch and the future looked bright once more with a new chairman, a new coach and even a new ground to call home.

2003: Challenge Cup Quarter-final

At the beginning of a new season it was reassuring to know that the Lions had returned close to the Swinton area for the first time since 1992. The Moor Lane ground is actually a significantly historic sporting venue. The ground once formed part of the Kersal Moor Racecourse which dates back to at least 1681 and was later known as Manchester Racecourse until 1847. From 1847 to 1919 the arena was home to Kersal Cricket club and from 1919 to 1968 it was home to Manchester Rugby Union Football Club, the oldest in the area having been formed in 1860, but currently playing at Grove Park in Cheadle Hulme close to the border with Cheshire. The currently tenants at Moor Lane are Salford City FC, but before that Langworthy Juniors Amateur Rugby League Football Club played there before moving to Pendlebury. It seemed the Lions were making progress as the Supporters' Trust sold plenty of 1960s replica Swinton shirts and even produced the retro-programme from the same period featuring a rampant Lion on the front cover.

The season started in earnest with a trip to the Willows in the National League Cup, after Salford had been relegated from Super League the previous season. Swinton were in the West Division but lost the opening fixture to the arch-rivals 58–6. The next match was in the third round of the Challenge Cup where the Lions beat Dewsbury amateurs Shaw Cross 46–0 in a game that included a try for Kris Tassell, an Australian signed from Wakefield Trinity after scoring 12 tries from 27 Super League games in 2002. The Lions lost at Leigh in the National League Cup before facing Chorley in the fourth round of the Challenge Cup at Victory Park. As a potential future money-spinner, this game was vital for both teams. When Swinton won 32–16 it was due mainly to a superb hat-tick from Kris Tassell as he proved his true value to the team. Another defeat in the National League Cup at home to Leigh was the prelude to an epic Challenge Cup encounter at Moor Lane.

National League One side Featherstone Rovers were the visitors in the fifth round as over 1,000 supporters attended the game. The Lions executed perfectly an exceptional game plan devised by Peter Roe who had a great ability to raise the game of many players especially on those all-important occasions. Swinton tackled well and frustrated the Rovers players and quickly established a lead through Phil Hassan, a former Leeds player, Jason Johnson and Wayne English. In the end, the Lions thoroughly deserved to win 32–10 even though

Rovers never stopped battling. Two Chris Hough drop-goals topped a great individual performance for the half-back who showed great tenacity all through the game. The entire squad of 17 players performed superbly and secured a passage to the quarter-final of the Challenge Cup for the first time since 1972. This was a truly outstanding achievement given the dire circumstance that the club faced less than a year before.

Swinton RLFC has had a long association with the Challenge Cup. The Lions first won the Challenge Cup in 1900 beating Salford 16–8 in the final at Fallowfield, Manchester. The Lions have lifted the cup three times winning again in 1926 and 1928 (the last final before the Wembley era). The club has been very unlucky in the cup too, in spite of having the players to win it especially in the glory days of the 1960s and early 1970s. So, to reach the quarter-final in 2003, the first time in over 30 years when beaten cruelly 9-8 at Halifax after knocking out holders Leigh in the second round, was quite an achievement by any standard. Actually, Swinton's finest post-war Challenge Cup achievement was reaching the semi-final against Wigan at St Helens in 1965. There was another notable cup run in 1971, which included a monumental 8-2 victory over Wigan at Station Road, but this too ended with a narrow 11-8 defeat in the quarter-final at Huddersfield.

In the 2003 Challenge Cup quarter-final, the Lions were drawn at home to Wigan. After much debate with the Wigan club, including some showmanship from the Wigan Chairman Maurice Lindsay, the tie was switched reluctantly to Wigan's JJB Stadium. Moor Lane could not hold safely many more than 1,000 spectators in any comfort and therefore was deemed unsuitable by the RFL. The Lions did have the option of playing at a neutral venue and ironically Gigg Lane would have been perfect to host the game. In fact, the largest attendance at Bury for a Swinton game was the second round of the defunct Lancashire Cup in September 1992 when Wigan won 78–0 in front of 3,501 spectators. On this occasion, the best option was to play the tie at the JJB Stadium although the Swinton coach Peter Roe knew there would have been a definite advantage for Swinton playing Wigan at Moor Lane on a sloping pitch and using small, basic changing rooms. In any event, frenzy in the media developed with articles about Swinton in national newspapers such as *The Independent* and *The Times* plus on BBC websites amid speculation that the club stood to gain anywhere between £17,500 to £35,000 from the cup tie with Wigan.

A crowd of 5,114 spectators arrived at Wigan to see the Lions play some spirited rugby league. Director Richard Taylor recalls there was a fantastic atmosphere on the Swinton team coach as many of the Lions players prepared for the most important match of their entire career. There were more than 1,000 Swinton fans in the away end at the JJB Stadium and doubtless others dotted around the ground. The years of hurt melted away as the Swinton supporters cheered and chanted in support of the Lions. The first quarter of the game was a very close affair with the Lions asking many questions of the Wigan players. Incredibly, Rob Russell gave the Lions the lead which was converted by Chris Hough and for a glorious few minutes the electronic scoreboard showed Swinton beating Wigan in the quarter-final of the Challenge Cup. Although Wigan regrouped and ran in several tries before half-time led ably by Adrian Lam, there was no doubt that the Swinton supporters had lived the dream. In the end, a late Andy Leathem try resulted in a final score of 70–12 in favour of Wigan, but the Lions had played with pride and tackled to a virtual standstill. Even at the very end of the game, Wayne English sprinted back in a vein attempt to tackle Wigan winger David Hodgson. As always, Wayne English personified the spirit in the Lions.

Back to the National League Cup, the Lions lost narrowly at Rochdale Hornets before crashing to a defeat at Leigh. There was a decent performance at home to Rochdale before another crushing defeat to Salford in an evening kick-off at Moor Lane. The immense high of the Wigan game was beginning to fade as another heavy defeat at Oldham followed and then a high scoring draw at home to Whitehaven brought an end to the extended National League Cup group stages. The Lions had played a lot of rugby league against quality opposition in a relatively short space of time which is a tall order for part-time players.

The National League Two season which replaced the NFP started with a good victory at home to Chorley in a game where Kris Smith, Lee Hudson and Jason Roach all performed well. An agonisingly close 8–4 defeat at Workington was cruel on the Lions; whereas a 35–38 defeat at home to Gateshead Thunder was not as the team from the North-East thoroughly deserved the win. Throughout the rest of May and early June, the Lions completed a tour of England. In order of matches played, there was a fine victory at Sheffield Eagles, a poor performance and defeat at York City Knights, a fine victory in London over the Skolars, where Wayne English was sent off and another defeat at Barrow Raiders. A 10–10 draw at home to Hunslet and a loss by three points at Keighley could both have been won with more clinical finishing although Kris Tassell, Jason Roach and Lee Hudson were all scoring tries with Chris Hough reliable as ever with the goal-kicking. At the Hunslet game there was a minute's silence for local author Bert Tyldesley MBE who had died recently at the age of 83. Bert was from Roe Green and a life-long Swinton supporter who had first watched the Lions at the Chorley Road ground in the late 1920s.

There were changes at the Supporters Trust with Steve Wild being replaced by Sue Buckley. Sue is a lifelong Swinton supporter and daughter of Alan Buckley, the stalwart star from the 1960s and early 1970s who was also honorary president of the Trust. Sue worked in the club shop on Station Road and provided a vital link between the supporters and the club at a crucial time when continuity was needed as much as anything else. Sue always works hard for the Swinton cause and has done so in many different capacities over a long period of time.

The Lions then hit a purple patch in July and won consecutive games for the first time in the season. Victories at home to Sheffield Eagles and Workington Town took place either side of a win at Gateshead Thunder. The Lions had the chances to win again at Chorley but lost before winning at home to London and York which could have delivered a six match winning run. As it happened five wins from six games was still the most consistent run of the season to date.

Swinton then run out of steam which is perhaps understandable given the exertions of the long season. The Lions lost convincingly at Hunslet before losing frustratingly by two points to Keighley; and then by four points to Barrow both at Moor Lane. The latter game proved to be the last ever Swinton game at Moor Lane just 13 months after arriving in Kersal. Around this time, Peter Roe left the club as head coach. By the end of the 2003 season, the Lions were on the move again this time back across the M62 motorway once more into the Metropolitan Borough of Bury, specifically to Whitefield and the home of Sedgley Park RUFC not far from Besses o' th' Barn metro station. This deal was brokered in part by Swinton directors Richard Taylor and Dave Jones along with Tony Griffin. The Park Lane ground offered improved facilities in every respect and much better prospects for the coming season. However, the Swinton club could have developed Moor Lane to the mutual benefit of both itself and Salford City FC.

In a season of high emotion and some exceptional achievement, the Swinton captain Simon Knox used his Super League experience gained at Halifax and Bradford to great effect and played in every single game marshalling superbly the young team. Chris Hough played with determination; and in the three-quarters Lee Hudson, Jason Roach and Kris Tassell collectively scored 42 tries in all competitions. Young players such as Rob Barraclough, Dave Ellison and Craig Wingfield all contributed well to the cause and Wayne English played 30 games scoring 16 tries. Furthermore, Wayne English and Chris Hough capped a fine season when they were both selected for a National League Two Select XIII to play against New Zealand 'A' at Keighley in October.

Finally, it is interesting to note that former Salford Corporation bought the Moor Lane ground from Manchester (Rugby Union) Football Club in 1968 for £57,000 which was a considerable sum of money at the time. However, in the final analysis the aspiration of Swinton Lions RLFC was ultimately higher than that of the host club in spite of Salford City FC being in turn a sub-tenant of Salford City Council. Unfortunately, there was a strong incumbency effect preventing any further development initiated by the Lions, which would have cost a great deal of money in any case. Nevertheless, this outcome was a missed opportunity for all concerned in the local community. The Moor Lane ground could have became a centre of multiple sporting uses and a facility for the whole area at all levels. As it was, the Lions moved reluctantly to Whitefield and the club was grateful to be welcomed at the ground of a rugby union club with sound facilities for the players, supporters and corporate clients alike. As for Wayne, his first five years in professional rugby league had been a steep learning curve on the pitch.

Leading the charge: Wayne sprints away from Oldham's Ricky Bibey.
27 February 2005 at Park Lane

Touch-down: Wayne English scores the first of two tries against Blackpool at Bloomfield Road, 5 March 2006

3. The second five years: 2004 to 2008

"I thought the players [against Sheffield Eagles] showed character to come back twice from behind to take the game by the scruff of the neck. It was good to have Wayne English and Lee Marsh back who had a big influence on the game along with Ian Watson."
Les Holliday (2005) writing in the Swinton programme

Introduction

Wayne had established himself in the first team during the first five years of his career. The next phase in any career is to cement that position. However, it was inevitable that Wayne would attract interest from other clubs having gained such rave reviews. The rugby league community is not vast in the National Leagues and opposition coaches and players alike are quick to spot the potential of any player either as a threat on the pitch or as a possible new signing. Yet Wayne was to remain loyal to Swinton and make the full-back berth his own over the next few seasons. However, before this was to happen the Lions had to make another move to Park Lane, a rugby union ground in Whitefield and home of Sedgley Park RUFC.

If the first five years of Wayne's time at Swinton had its share of wandering about Greater Manchester in search of a new ground, both permanent and temporary, then the next five years was marked by relative stability. The venue at Park Lane was to be Swinton's new home for the years ahead in spite of Salford RLFC following the Lions to Whitefield and using the facilities as a training base; not to mention Oldham RLFC using the ground for occasional matches when the Boundary Park pitch was being reseeded in the summer. The Park Lane ground has a compact main stand and good hospitality facilities in a clubhouse typical of many rugby union clubs in the area and similar to Manchester RUFC or Macclesfield RUFC. The pitch is a huge playing surface with a deceptive slope heading down from the clubhouse. The other notable thing about the pitch is the enormous in-goal areas - seldom used in rugby union, of course.

2004: Arriving at Whitefield

Another ground move for Swinton RLFC was the last thing the club wanted, but in the end there was no point in remaining at Moor Lane. Although the ground at Kersal was less than a mile from the Borough of Swinton and Pendlebury border and within sight of the Cusssons soap factory which originated in Swinton, it remained a largely uninspiring place to play rugby league even for the Lions. Actually, Park Lane is not too far from Swinton and Pendlebury either. The top of the Sedgley Park floodlights are just visible from the M60 as you drive through the Irwell Valley. On one side of the carriageway is Pilkington's Tile factory, home of the famous Lancaster Pottery as well as the Clifton Bridge, with a magnificent span of 13 arches, and on the other side is Phillips Park part of the altogether leafier suburb of Whitefield. Indeed, from the Sedgley Park second team pitches further down Park Lane there are magnificent views across the Borough of Swinton and Pendlebury. The rows of terraced houses are visible clearly along with the mills and factories. This is the exact scene that inspired L.S. Lowry to paint industrial landscapes when he lived in Swinton and Pendlebury from 1909 to 1948. He lived for the majority of this time on Station Road and was a neighbour to the Lions when the club moved from the Chorley Road ground in 1929. In fact, Lowry produced much of his critically acclaimed work of composite working class scenes such as the Acme Mill in Pendlebury and Clifton Colliery while living on Station Road.

The 2004 season began with a tough series of games that would test severely the character of newly appointed coach Paul Kidd. Paul, a lifelong Swinton supporter who has served the club in many previous capacities including commercial manager, formed part of the partnership that effectively saved the club in 2002 along with the Supporters' Trust. Paul took on a massive role at the club, although he was supported by Swinton legend Les Holliday as director of rugby. Nevertheless, this was a huge responsibility for Paul given that he is the son of John Kidd, the Swinton chairman. John Kidd's passion for Swinton dates back to 1947 when he first watched the Lions play at Station Road and there is no doubting the commitment of both Paul and John to the Swinton cause. On the playing front, the Lions signed Swinton-based winger Chris Irwin, powerful prop Tau Liku from Barrow, Paul Ashton and Ian Sinfield both from Keighley as well re-signed former players Neil Hayden, Wes Rogers and Ryan Stazicker.

The first match at Park Lane was a tough encounter in the National League Cup against a well-organised and a well-drilled Leigh side that brought a big following with them. A decent crowd of 1,351 crammed into Park Lane as the Lions competed well but eventually went down 22–6. A well taken try by Chris Maye was the only reward for Swinton on the occasion of Park Lane hosting its first ever game of professional rugby league. Interestingly, the ground itself was acquired by Sedgley Park from the Co-operative movement with the main use for recreational purposes.

The next game at Park Lane was a disaster as the Lions' long and proud record over 100 years of never losing to amateur clubs in the Challenge Cup came to an abrupt end. East Hull, an amateur team from East Yorkshire, put in a determined display in murky conditions and simply deserved to win 26–14. Hull is a hot-bed of rugby league and the area has provided many talented players for the game. It was a tough blow for Swinton and their supporters not least when a spot of trouble in the main stand threatened to spoil the excellent albeit fledgling relationship with Sedgley Park.

As for Swinton head coach Paul Kidd, he was having a very tough baptism in the uncompromising world of professional rugby league. Things did not improve immediately for the Lions' young coach. A long trip to Whitehaven in the National League Cup saw a defeat; followed by another loss at home to Oldham. Then the Lions won finally at home to Chorley, but only 27–24. The tries from Jason Roach, Chris Irwin and Peter Cannon among others were to prove vital for the Lions.

Next the Lions received a lesson in clinical rugby league at Hilton Park as Leigh stormed home by 66–6. A further two defeats to Oldham and Chorley, respectively completed a miserable start to the season even though the full league campaign had not begun. However, there were some positive signs for the Lions' coaching staff. Chris Irwin and Chris Maye were scoring tries and Phil Cushion and Danny Heaton were performing well in the pack. Also, Wayne English was playing as well as ever in the full-back role.

The indifferent start to the season in the National League Cup was transformed by some much-improved performances when the National League Two season began in earnest. The first game at home to Gateshead Thunder witnessed some excellent play as the Lions won 42–10. The Lions then secured an impressive win at Dewsbury inspired by two tries from Peter Cannon. The team followed this performance with the biggest win of the season at home to Workington Town 64–26. A Wayne English hat-trick, the first in his professional career, was the highlight of the match along with nine goals from half-back Paul Ashton.

The Lions were top of the table after the opening three games and beginning to make progress under the new coaching team. Inexplicably there then followed a mini-slump as Swinton lost the next four games. A defeat at Hunslet in a tough encounter was followed by a heavy 46–10 loss at home to Barrow. Two further away trips ended in defeat against York and London Skolars. At this time the Lions were forging stronger links with local Rugby League Conference side Bolton Le Moor.

The Lions had dropped to fifth place but the slump was corrected with spirited performances that realised wins at home to Chorley, at Sheffield and a fine win at home to Dewsbury. Paul Ashton performed particularly well in the latter game with a try and five goals. The long trek to Workington ended the run of victories as the Cumbrian team was beginning to improve vastly in the second part of the season.

The Lions then revenged the defeats by Hunslet and Barrow with victories over both clubs. In a thrilling game at Park Lane, Swinton beat Hunslet 33–16 and at

Craven Park the Lions beat Barrow 20–12. Remarkably, the final league defeat of the season followed as York completed the double over the Lions inflicting a heavy defeat at Park Lane.

The Lions then won the final four league games. London Skolars were beaten and then the short trip along the A6 to Victory Park, Chorley also ended in a Swinton win, which guaranteed the Lions a play-off spot. Wes Rogers and Ian Hodson were performing well in the pack, while Wayne English scored a try in four consecutive games. Sheffield Eagles were beaten at home before the final long trip of the season to play Gateshead Thunder saw the Lions squeeze home by 28–23 following a spirited performance by the home side. Utility back Safraz Patel played exceptionally well during this period as did back-row forward Rob Russell who contributed with some fine goal-kicking in addition.

Although Swinton finished in fourth place, the Lions were arguably the form team with nine wins in the final 11 games. The damage to the league campaign had been caused during an indifferent spell of four defeats part way through the season. Nevertheless, the Lions were rightly confident of a good play-off series in September. The Elimination play-off paired Swinton at home to Workington Town, a team that had improved vastly since May when the Lions scored over 60 points against them. The game was anticipated eagerly and Town brought a sizeable contingent in the crowd of 768. In a very close encounter Town edged it by six points in a game where the lead changed several times. Swinton scored eight tries but this was not quite enough as Workington claimed victory with some sterling defence as the Lions played catch-up rugby. In spite of the obvious disappointment, the Lions had recovered well from the shock cup exit and poor displays in the National League Cup to finish the season with a very credible league campaign.

Overall, the Swinton club was making the most of their new surroundings in Whitefield. The Lions have been always regarded as the Manchester club in rugby league circles and it is fitting that Manchester City Centre is visible from the main-stand at Sedgley Park against a background of the Pennines. The Lions were beginning to feel at home in their new setting. Another change during the season had come in March when Martin McDonough became chairman of the Supporters' Trust.

2005: Making an impact
Wayne had a great season in 2004 and he was on an upward curve. 2005 was to be another successful season for him and the Lions with many exciting games and some great play by the entire team. The lesson from the previous season was that during a relatively short league season of 18 matches, there was no margin for error and consistency is the key to success. The Lions did have a

tight-knit squad with players of genuine pace including Lee Patterson and Wayne English. There were other players with great power and strength including Marlon Billy who had rejoined the club and Phil Joseph who had recently signed from Huddersfield.

The season began well with victories in the first five encounters which supported the claims from head-coach Paul Kidd that the season would be a positive one. The Lions started the campaign with a sound victory over Rochdale Hornets at Park Lane in the National League Cup knock-out stages, group two. This was followed up with victories against newly-formed Blackpool Panthers at the developing Bloomfield Road stadium and a hard-earned double over Oldham. The 46–14 victory over National League One side Oldham at Park Lane was particularly impressive and included a Wayne English hat-trick. A week later the Lions again beat Oldham, this time at Boundary Park, 37–30.

Swinton were then paired at home with Russian champions Locomotiv Moscow in the third round of the Challenge Cup. It was a genuine honour for the club to host rugby league pioneers and a great opportunity to help establish the game in Russia. The harsh Russian winters meant that the Moscow players could not train outdoors until they arrived in England. Locomotiv are the most successful team in the Russian domestic competition and like the Lions were formed originally as a rugby union club before switching to rugby league. As for the game, the Lions won comfortably 70–10 including a splendid four-try haul for Chris Maye. To hear players calling out moves and instructions in Russian during a game against Swinton was wonderful. It would have been unimaginable a decade before, never mind in 1866, that the Lions would one day be playing a team from Russia in a cup competition. Interestingly, this match was covered by the television cameras from Channel M, a free-to-air television station for Manchester.

The following week the Lions returned to domestic action in the National League Cup against Rochdale Hornets for a rivalry that dates all the way back to 1871. Swinton lost heavily and then inexplicably drew the next match at home to Blackpool Panthers. The Panthers deserved the result and included several former Swinton players including Danny Barton, Chris Hough and Jake Johnstone in their squad. Nevertheless, and in spite of the indifferent finish to the National League Cup group stages, the Lions had reached the qualifying play-offs.

The league season opened with a tough victory away to York City Knights who had been progressing well since reforming following the collapse of the former York club. During the game, the Lions returned to some fine form as half-backs Mick Coates and Ian Watson were outstanding, as was loose-forward Lee Marsh who was fulfilling his potential with displays that combined strength of a forward and the guile of a half-back as well as a good approach to goalkicking. Subsequent events proved that this result would be one of the best all season, but for now the Lions were content with starting the all important league campaign in style.

If the Lions had played against novel opposition from Moscow in the third round of the Challenge Cup, then in the fourth round it was all too familiar opponents from Widnes. For many older Swinton supporters, Widnes is regarded as something of a difficult team for the Lions to knock-out of the Challenge Cup as a result of several narrow defeats over the years after replays especially in the 1960s. The Vikings, coached by Kiwi Frank Endacott, had won twice already in Super League X and would prove tough opposition at the Halton Stadium. The Swinton supporters provided vocal support in the crowd of 2,263 and the team responded well to playing against higher level opposition. In the first half the Lions acquitted themselves well and trailed by 16–12 at the interval. Two Marlon Billy tries and a solo effort from Phil Joseph were not enough as the home side won eventually 32–18, but the Lions were far from disgraced with Danny Heaton and Phil Joseph in the pack and Lee Patterson in the threequarters playing exceptionally well and on a par with their opposite number. In the years following this encounter several players in the Widnes squad have gone on to join the Lions including Paul Alcock, Paul Crook, Gary Hulse, Bruce Johnson and Darren Woods.

The Lions returned to league action with a comfortable home win against Workington Town followed by a shock heavy reverse at Dewsbury where two Danny Heaton tries were not enough as the Lions went down 48–10 in an instantly forgettable Swinton display. The shock was the margin of defeat not the loss, but the Lions had to regroup as quickly as possible. A visit to the capital saw the Lions bounce back against London Skolars before a home game in the National League Cup against Batley. Having performed so poorly against Dewsbury a couple of weeks before, the transformation against the other part of the Heavy Woollens district of West Yorkshire could not have been more dramatic. Swinton played exceptionally effective rugby league against National League One Batley. Once more Ian Watson excelled at half-back and the pace of Lee Patterson netted him a hat-trick as the Lions won 40–24.

The following week the Lions continued their impressive form beating Blackpool 82–12 at Park Lane including another Patterson hat-tick and a brace for Wayne English. Two Mick Coates tries secured a win the following week at Keighley as the Lions were starting to gain momentum. The next match was the quarter-final of the National League Cup and the Lions were handed the dubious honour of a trip to east Hull to face in form Hull KR.

Even at the end of May, Humberside can seem like an inhospitable place and so it proved for Swinton and not for the first time. New Craven Park is devoid of charm for any opposition and this occasion was no exception as the Robins and their vociferous support lay in wait for the arrival of the Lions from across the Pennines. The Hull KR coach, Harvey Howard, devised a plan to blunt the Swinton attacking options while at the same time put pressure on the Lions' defensive line from the kick-off. The Rovers players executed the game plan to perfection as the Lions went down 62–0. Scrum-half Phil Hasty had a field day scoring a hat-trick of tries and Gareth Morton kicked nine goals as Hull KR played some of their best rugby of the season to date. Inexplicably Rovers parted company with Harvey Howard a few weeks later and replaced him with a young Australian coach named Justin Morgan just after they had beaten Castleford in the National League Cup Final at Blackpool.

The mauling at Hull KR seemed to knock a lot of confidence out of the Lions who until that point had beaten three National League One sides and performed so well at Super League Widnes. The aftermath proved critical as the Lions lost four of the next five league games. A narrow defeat at Hunslet was not totally unexpected but shipping 57 points at home to Gateshead in the following game was a surprise. Victory over Sheffield Eagles at Park Lane steadied the nerves before another defeat at Workington followed by one at home to York began to seriously undermine the entire season. Of course, success can lead to more success, but the National League Cup run was beginning to adversely affect the important league campaign.

The Lions did rally in July with victories at Blackpool and at home to London Skolars and Hunslet. However, another poor display on the east coast followed with a 58–10 defeat against improving Gateshead Thunder. The Gateshead club was making huge strides under head coach Dean Thomas, a former player at York and Barrow, and nothing should be taken away from the Thunder's performance because the team eventually made the play-offs for the first time, completing a double over the Lions in the process.

The Lions then put in a great display at home to Keighley winning 46–0. This was followed by a good win at Sheffield over the Eagles before losing at home to Dewsbury by only four points. This ended the regular league season with the Lions finishing in fourth position. There was disappointment in the Swinton camp with this outcome, especially considering the great start and the fine displays in cup competitions - with the notable exception of the Hull KR result. In a league with only 10 teams too many unexpected defeats are punished and the Lions lost seven games in total, four more than champions York City Knights.

Nevertheless, the Lions had reached the play-offs and faced Hunslet in the Elimination play-off at Park Lane. Hunslet and Swinton have much in common. Both are proud towns in large conurbations and have won all the available trophies in a single season: Hunslet in 1907–08 and Swinton in 1927–28. In a mid-September clash, the Lions finished on top 40–28 but nothing should be taken away from the gutsy performance by Hunslet who were always in contention until late in the game. A try each for Chris Maye, Ian Parry, Lee Marsh, Danny Heaton, Andy Crabtree, Lee Patterson and Wayne English clinched the game for Swinton along with a grafting display from Paul Southern and Ian Sinfield in the pack, who is elder brother of Leeds international star Kevin.

The Elimination semi-final play-off at Workington Town was an even closer affair. Tries from Marlon Billy and Dave Llewellyn plus four Lee Marsh goals were cancelled out by three Town tries and two Jon Roper goals. In the end, the difference that separated the teams on the day was a Lee Kiddie drop-goal for Town that meant heartbreak for the Lions. During the league season, third-placed Workington had been more consistent and lost only four games and drawn one. Workington Town then lost to Dewsbury in the Final Eliminator. In turn, Dewsbury were beaten by Batley in the Final; and so it was Batley who retained National League One status, a team that the Lions had beaten convincingly earlier in the season.

Although the season was ultimately disappointing, the Lions had played some exciting rugby league. The emphasis on scoring tries had paid dividends with four players totalling 20 or more touchdowns apiece, namely, Marlon Billy (26), Wayne English (25), Lee Marsh (20) and Lee Patterson (21). Lee Marsh also kicked 114 goals plus 2 drop-goals giving him an impressive total of 310 points for the season the most by a Swinton player since Albert Blan at the start of the halcyon days of the 1960–61 season. Furthermore, Wayne English, Marlon Billy, Lee Marsh and Phil Joseph were all named in the *Rugby League World* All-Star Team for National League Two. Off the field, the Supporters' Trust had set-up a sub-committee known as M27 Stadium Community Project to investigate ways to return the club to Swinton and Pendlebury, including a site at Wardley. Also, John Kidd announced a Foundation aimed at raising the profile of the club. Finally, the death was announced of George Jones, a stalwart of the back-room staff for many years at Station Road.

2006: Grand Final
The previous season had seen success on and off the field for the Lions, but there was a general feeling that the team had actually under-achieved. In fairness it is possible that the 2006 season could have been regarded as unfulfilled potential had it not been for an inspiring end to the campaign. All this was in the future, but there was a genuine sense of optimism at Swinton in spite

of losing Lee Marsh - albeit he returned later - and Danny Heaton both to Widnes; Phil Joseph to Hull KR plus the retirement of Chris Irwin. The club made some very useful acquisitions including utility player Liam McGovern from Blackpool Panthers, the vastly experienced Kiwi Martin Moana and an exciting prospect on the wing, Andy Saywell.

The season started well enough with an excellent display at the Halton Stadium in the National League Cup (Group Four) against a much-fancied Widnes team from National League One that contained a great deal of Super League experience with players such as Mick Cassidy, Denis Moran, Terry O'Connor and Mark Smith. Also, there were a fair number of former Swinton players at Widnes as well including the much-travelled Mick Nanyn, Danny Heaton and Lee Marsh. In a closely fought game the Lions performed well, frustrating the home team and even played some good rugby in a match that could have gone either way. As it was Widnes won 18–10 in front of an impressive attendance of 3,887. For Swinton, Liam McGovern made a great debut at hooker and Ian Parry scored a well deserved try.

Blackpool Panthers were beaten at home in the next game followed by a close defeat at home to Leigh, another National League One side. The visiting team was led ably by the experienced Paul Rowley, but Ian Watson performed well keeping the Lions in the game with a try and a goal before Leigh eventually won 30–20. Swinton won at Bloomfield Road against Blackpool Panthers before adverse weather forced the postponement of the third round Challenge Cup at home to Sheffield Eagles. The match was rearranged for the following Tuesday, but was still played in terribly wet conditions, especially in the second half. The match was keenly fought, but the Lions eventually were convincing 42–18 winners, including a Wayne English hat-trick. The delayed match under heavy conditions took its toll on the Swinton players and five days later the team crashed to a heavy defeat against Widnes at Park Lane.

In a remarkable turnaround, the following week the Lions went to Hilton Park and won 18–14 against Leigh. In a really great team effort Swinton won the game with tries from Andy Saywell, Mike Stout and Wayne English plus three goals from Kris Smith. This victory established the Lions as a team that could beat any other National League side. However, there remained the unresolved issue of consistency as the team crashed out of the Challenge Cup in the fourth round to York City Knights 20–18 the following week. Although York had won promotion to National League One the previous season, the manner in which the City Knights players celebrated victory after the final hooter suggested that they had not expected to win at Park Lane. This match also marked the final Swinton appearance for Jordon James who signed for Wigan on 7 April, reminiscent of Dave Robinson who made the same move in 1970, albeit as an Great Britain international. James, a former Royal Marine who had served in Iraq, went straight into the Wigan side crushed by St Helens on Good Friday. James did a remarkable job at Wigan scoring three Super League tries in only two starts plus four more games as substitute before moving on again to Widnes in National League One prior to the end of the season.

Then the Lions won three games on the trot, beating Barrow and Blackpool Panthers at home and winning in London against the Skolars. The National League Cup quarter-final qualifier at Workington was the next fixture. Derwent Park has never been a successful venue for the Lions and so it proved again as they went down 46–30, in spite of a couple of tries each for inspirational leader Martin Moana and Darren Woods plus one for Dave Ashton (brother of Wigan's Chris Ashton).

A narrow victory at home to Gateshead Thunder saw Lee Marsh cap a fine individual performance with a try and five goals to put the Lions top of the National League Two table. There followed another trek to Workington in the league and another agonising defeat by a narrow margin of five points. Yet another long trip to Cumbria the following week yielded a better outcome in very wet conditions. In a close game at Barrow in which both defences dominated, the Lions were losing by eight points late in the game when first Marlon Billy intercepted and raced into score; and then David Alstead slide in from several metres out to clinch the game. The next game at home to title contenders Dewsbury would be crucial. In a game where the lead changed hands several times, the Lions outscored the Rams by four tries to three. However, the visitors scored five goals to one to win the game in the dying seconds of the contest following a mistake on the Swinton try-line by Wayne English when he dropped the ball. Dewsbury gained top spot in the table after this result and this impetus gave the Yorkshire team a huge boost in race for the title.

The Lions then won convincingly at Blackpool against the Panthers before a home match with Hunslet staged at the Willows because Park Lane was unavailable. This happened five years earlier in 2001 by coincidence against the same opponents when the Lions were based at Gigg Lane. The staging of this match caused the Swinton-Salford ground-sharing debate to resurface, albeit briefly. Salford were planning to move to a new purpose-built stadium close to Barton aerodrome across the Manchester Ship Canal from the Trafford Centre Shopping Complex. At the time, it seemed likely that when they relocate from The Willows it would be developed for key-worker housing and so a long-term move to the ground was not viable in any case. The Lions won the game itself 54–22, although Lee Marsh was badly injured following a challenge from a Hunslet player.

The Lions' title challenge was dealt another blow when the Celtic Crusaders, a newly-formed team from South Wales, won convincingly 50–18 at Park Lane. A narrow defeat the following week at Featherstone sent the Lions to fifth place in the league. Albert Blan was the Swinton captain the last time the Lions had won at Post Office Road in 1964 and it seemed they were destined never to win at Featherstone again.

A well deserved victory at home to Workington followed. Then came an unexpected win in Bridgend against Celtic Crusaders, who had been previously undefeated at home in the league. The Lions won 21–10 due in part to a great defensive display in sweltering temperatures, which caused many of the players to suffer from heat exhaustion. The Lions were back up to third in the league.

Midway through the season there was a significant change in playing personnel. Influential scrum-half Ian Watson left to join Widnes, as Jordon James had done earlier via Wigan, and in the opposite direction arrived prolific try scorer Darren Woods, hooker Phil Wood and prop Bruce Johnson - who had played under former Swinton coach Mike Gregory in the Great Britain Academy team - all initially on-loan.

The next few fixtures proved frustrating for the Lions. In July, the club lost home and away to Sheffield Eagles in the league. In between these fixtures the team beat Featherstone Rovers at home with tries from newcomers Bruce Johnson and Phil Wood. The first defeat to Sheffield Eagles ended a seven-match winning streak over the South Yorkshire team just when many at the Don Valley Stadium were beginning to think that Swinton were their bogey side.

The Lions achieved a 24–24 draw at Hunslet; the highlight of which was the one and only try in Swinton colours for on loan giant Cook Island international Tama Wakelin. This was a rescheduled fixture because on the original date the Hunslet club doctor did not attend and under RFL rules the match had to be postponed. Final notice of the cancellation arrived about 15 minutes after the scheduled kick-off time leaving the Swinton officials, players and supporters very unhappy. When the match was finally played many Lions supporters arrived in white doctors' coats. The defeat at Keighley in the next game was seen by many as the worst display of the entire season. Next came a victory over London Skolars, but this was followed by defeat at Dewsbury which all but condemned the Lions to fifth spot and helped the Rams on their way to the National League Two title. At this time, the East Lancashire Lions, a club with links to Swinton and based at Darwen FC, played South London Storm in the Rugby League Conference Grand Final at Coventry.

Next, there followed a quite remarkable series of games as good as any involving a Swinton team for a very long time indeed. First, the Lions avenged the defeat at Keighley by beating them 54–10 at Park Lane including a hat-trick of tries for Andy Saywell. Then the Lions won on Tyneside against Gateshead Thunder, which is never an easy place to win in, and thereby confirmed fifth position in the league. This was something of a disappointment given the calibre of the team and some fine performances, especially at Brewery Field against Celtic Crusaders.

The Lions won the third of three encounters during the season against Barrow at Park Lane in the Elimination play-off 26–20. Darren Woods continued his impressive try-scoring run with two more to add to his tally. History was made when the Lions won finally at Featherstone in the Elimination semi-final. There was a large Swinton following among the crowd of 1,205 as the Lions slowly, but surely, dominated the game winning 27–14. Every player in the team from number one to seventeen in the Swinton line-up contributed to the victory. In particular, Kris Smith and Lee Marsh played well in the pack with Darren Woods and Andy Saywell running well down the flanks. In truth, the Lions deserved to win and out-played Rovers, but having not won in this corner of Yorkshire for so long no-one in Swinton colours took anything for granted. There were great scenes of jubilation when the final hooter sounded, even though victory meant another trip to South Wales. For the record, the last Swinton team to leave victorious from Post Office Road was on 27 February 1964 when a Ken Halliwell try and three goals from Ken Gowers inspired the Lions to a 9–2 victory in the Challenge Cup. The Swinton team coach had broken down on the way to the ground and Albert Blan had predicted this unusual event would prove to be a lucky omen. Over 40 years later, Swinton had no such bad fortune on the way over the Pennines, but the Lions had the same resolve to triumph in a cup game.

One week later, the Lions were making the long trek to Bridgend for the Final Eliminator. The task ahead of the team was daunting. Celtic had home advantage and two extra days to prepare having lost narrowly to Sheffield Eagles on Friday evening the previous weekend. The Crusaders had also hammered the Lions at Park Lane earlier in the season, scoring 50 points in the process. What followed will be part of Swinton folklore for a long time. In a truly even contest both teams threw everything at each other in what was one of the best games of rugby league to feature Swinton in almost 40 years. Tries from Paul Alcock, Darren Woods, Lee Marsh and Liam McGovern seemed insufficient as the Crusaders were still in the lead late in the game. Then a superb McGovern-inspired try and conversion by Lee Marsh levelled the score at 26–26. A further two periods of 10 minutes extra-time produced no further score which forced the match into golden-point territory. As the game restarted, Swinton gained possession and Phil Wood made a decisive break down Swinton's right flank. Although he was tackled within touching distance of the Celtic try-line he had done the damage as a tackle later and 91 seconds after the final passage of play began, Chris Hough sent over a drop-goal and scored a golden point for the first time in the history of professional rugby league in Britain. The place erupted and Swinton fans, vocal throughout the game swarmed onto the pitch in a good natured, but ecstatic, way. Even BBC Radio Manchester commentator, Phil Kinsella described the game as "the most dramatic victory I have ever, ever seen." In truth, no team deserved to lose and the players and supporters of Celtic accepted this most cruel form of defeat in a dignified and sporting way. As for Swinton, they were heading for the Grand Final at Warrington against Sheffield Eagles. The celebrations lasted well into the night as Swinton had secured another famous victory on the road.

The last time that Swinton had reached a divisional final was back in May 1989 and they had also faced Sheffield Eagles at Old Trafford. Ominously, the Eagles won that afternoon in Manchester, but perhaps more significantly the South Yorkshire side had broken a long run of consecutive Swinton victories earlier in the season. Nevertheless, Swinton approached the game in confident mood buoyed by the fact that in the first encounter between the teams in February the Lions had won 42–18. Swinton took a following of 1,000 supporters to Warrington and there was genuine excitement as the club appeared on the BBC Television regional news programme *Look North-West* on the Monday evening before the final, which included footage of the drop-goal against Celtic and the post-match celebrations on the pitch.

Sheffield Eagles were to prove a stern test for Swinton. The Eagles had made a superb end-of-season run including the play-offs and prior to the Grand Final had won their previous 12 games under former Hull KR coach Gary Wilkinson. The early part of the contest was even and a Rob Worrincy try was cancelled out by a try from Andy Saywell. However, two quick tries by the Eagles minutes before half-time undid a great deal of hard work as the Lions struggled to remain in contention. Three more tries in the second half for Sheffield confirmed their superiority and a late try for Dave Alstead wonderfully crafted by Wayne English was in the end only a consolation. The game ended with the Eagles winning 35–10, similar to the final in 1989 that ended 43–18 in favour of the men from the steel city. There was disappointment for the Lions as well as a great sense of achievement, not least for Wayne English as his tackling and relentless spirit earned him a rave review and the man-of-the-match award. Coach Paul Kidd was gracious in defeat and cited individual errors as the cause of the defeat and not fatigue. Later the same day there was also disappointment for two former Lions who had begun the season at Park Lane; namely Jordon James and Ian Watson who played for Widnes in their National League One Grand Final defeat to Super League-bound Hull KR.

For many informed observers, Swinton had the potential to secure promotion in the 2005 campaign and to be so near the following season was another measure of progress. In the *Rugby League World* All Star team Marlon Billy and Martin Moana were selected. In the end, Sheffield Eagles deserved to win the Grand Final and Dewsbury deserved to lift the National League Two title. The Lions played their part too and generated some wonderful memories, especially at Brewery Field. The Grand Final was exciting to witness and Wayne English in particular played the best game of his Swinton career even in defeat, which is often a sign of an outstanding player. Around this time, there was even news that the club had entered in negotiations with Salford City Council about a proposed new ground in Agecroft at the Pendlebury end of the Borough. On the downside, at the end of the season director of rugby Les Holliday left the club.

2007: Consolidating at Park Lane
The season following the Grand Final was always going to be a tough one for the club not least because there were higher expectations of the players. The experience of a major showpiece event at a Super League stadium with Sky Television coverage was wonderful for everyone especially given the dramatic way by which the team clinched a place in the final. However, a Boxing Day friendly at Leigh did not bode well for the new season as an unfamiliar looking Lions were mauled 50–0 by an effective home side. The euphoria of the Grand Final remained in evidence around the club, but there were changes afoot on the playing front. By the end of the season many of the players in the 2006 squad had left and even some of those drafted in to replace them had also departed by the end of the campaign. In particular, John Walker on a season-long loan from Wigan only played a handful of games and Mark Ogden, an Australian who signed for the Lions after being released from Oldham, similarly made a total of only five appearances. Other new arrivals included former St Helens Academy player Craig Ashall, Rob Line from Gateshead Thunder and Mike Smith, nephew of Kris Smith and a former player at Folly Lane ARLFC. Several players left the club before the start of the season including Ian Sinfield and Kris Smith to Oldham and David Alstead to Leigh.

As it happened, the season began relatively well in February with victories over Hunslet at Park Lane and Oldham at Boundary Park both in the National League Cup. These matches were the first two in a round robin mini-league (Group Four) that also included Rochdale Hornets. Each team played the others on a home and way basis. A disappointing reverse at home to Rochdale was followed by a creditable 10–10 draw at Hunslet in a keenly fought encounter. The next visitors to Park Lane were Locomotiv Moscow for the second time in three years for a third round Challenge Cup tie. The Lions ran out comfortable winners, 60–20 in front a rather low crowd of 331 fans. It remains an ambition of the Rugby

Football League (RFL) to expand the game as far and wide as possible and the evidence of this policy is found in initiatives such as inviting Russian and French teams to participate in the early rounds of the prestigious Challenge Cup. As for the Russians, on this occasion they viewed the result as an improvement on their previous visit to Park Lane when Swinton won by 70–10. The Lions played good albeit unspectacular rugby but it has to be remembered that the Locomotiv players cannot prepare for the game on grass such is the severity of the winter in Russia. It remains a truly memorable sporting occasion for the club to host a team from Moscow and an honour to help the game develop internationally. Given that the club travelled domestically as far as Workington, Gateshead, London and Bridgend in the 2007 season then maybe the expansion beyond the M62 corridor was finally happening. In any case, there is no disputing that this division is truly national and the Challenge Cup truly international.

Back in the National League Cup, the Lions finished the group stages in worrying fashion conceding 42 points to both Rochdale at Spotland and Oldham at Park Lane. The latter match was the first victory for Oldham against professional opposition in over a year and this defeat was compounded by the fact two former Swinton players from the previous season scored a try for Oldham, Ian Sinfield and Kris Smith. In spite of these results the Lions finished second in Group Four and gained a place in the Qualifying quarter-final round. Also, in March, Swinton's new Academy side was established with high hopes of supplying future first-team players as happened in the 1990s. Ian Wade, a life-long Swinton supporter with strong links to local amateur rugby league, was installed as Academy head coach.

The Lions next returned to the Challenge Cup against fellow National League Two opposition. The home tie against Barrow represented a winnable match for the Lions, but the visitors executed a near perfect game plan under the guidance of half-back Darren Holt. The only highlight of the game for Swinton was the performance of local player Mike Smith who continued to impress with some hard work in the pack. The Lions then travelled to the seaside for the opening National League fixture against Blackpool Panthers. It was their first visit since the team relocated to the ground of Fylde RUFC in Lytham. The facilities at the ground included a really excellent new clubhouse incorporating changing rooms and restaurant as well as old wooden stand down one side that would not have looked out of place 100 years ago. In a close game the Lions snatched victory in the dying seconds due in part to a hat-tick from London-born wingman Desi Williams. The next league game was against Barrow, coincidently a fortnight after the cup defeat. This gave the Lions an opportunity to show there had been improvement and the team responded in spite of another defeat this time by the slender margin of 35–30. Wayne English scored twice in this game and showed some really good touches when in possession of the ball.

There was another repeat of a result this time as the Lions lost again at Rochdale in the National League Cup quarter-final qualifier at Spotland, albeit by the narrower margin of 30–16. The Hornets were a division higher than the Lions, but these are the yardsticks by which any team should be tested. By the end of the season, Rochdale Hornets were relegated and their final game was a 106–0 defeat at home to Super League bound Castleford.

It was back to league for the Lions and the long trip down to the Brewery Field in South Wales to play Celtic Crusaders. This was the third trip to the principality for the Lions in less than a year, having not previously played in Wales since 1996. The game itself was a lesson in creative play and finishing power for Swinton as Celtic gained ample revenge for the Grand Final Eliminator defeat. The Lions were hammered 82–4, which marked a genuine low point in the season, not least for the poor tackling. The Celtic supporters in the bar afterwards were very sporting as they had been in defeat twice the previous season. Interestingly, one the Celtic supporters included Kenny Roberts, former chairman of Eccles ARLFC and one-time contributor to the Swinton match-day programme who travels to every Celtic game home and away from Eccles.

One great aspect of sport is that you have the opportunity to start at nil-nil in every game no matter what the result of the previous encounter. And so the Lions were able to start the next game against a useful Gateshead team with a clean sheet in spite of the crushing defeat to Celtic. Remarkably, the Lions won 58–12, including a brace of tries from Marlon Billy and the one and only try in the brief Swinton career of Mark Ogden who soon after returned to his native Australia. This showed what the team could do on the pitch, but also identified a level of inconsistency, not least as the Lions lost the next game at home to York in a fixture the team had a good chance of winning.

The Lions travelled to two tough away games in the height of the summer at Barrow and Featherstone and lost both in spite of beating both these teams in the play-offs at the end of the previous season. A narrow victory at Hunslet, orchestrated by the superb kicking game of Liam McGovern, was followed by another good win at Park Lane over Keighley. The winning run ended in the capital against an improving London Skolars team under the astute stewardship of Kiwi coach Latham Tawhai. The following week the Lions were at the other end of the county playing at Workington's Derwent Park. This match was the fifth away trip in six games, and the Lions lost agonisingly 38–33 after a disputed late try for the home side.

During this period the club was docked six league points for entering administration midway through the season. The same punishment was metered-out to National League One club Doncaster for the same offence. The Swinton directors have always insisted that the measure was taken to help the club re-organise and not to benefit the team on the pitch as is often the case with a club going into administration. In any case, the period of administration lasted only a matter of days, but the RFL did not change its mind and so this decision undid much good work by the players on the field of play, where league points are actually won. Interestingly, Swinton had been docked league points before, two points in the 1898–99 season and four in the 1901–02 season, on both occasions for breaches of the rules about professionalism.

Three good displays followed starting with a win at home against Oldham due again in part to the kicking game of Liam McGovern. There was also some restored credibility after a narrow defeat to Celtic by only six points. Another lengthy road trip followed this time to the north east to play Gateshead Thunder. A great win was secured in the second half with a brace of tries by Chris Hull and a powerful display by former Castleford and Warrington prop David Bates. However, a disappointing display at Keighley and a closely fought game at home to Featherstone both ended in defeat.

Swinton then enjoyed a mini-revival. Blackpool Panthers, coached by former Wigan great Andy Gregory, were beaten convincingly at Park Lane 70–20, including two tries each for Wayne English, Rob Line, Phil Wood and Andy Saywell. Next came a really great victory at York, in which quicksilver Phil Wood was taken out having released the ball in a perfectly timed pass to Lee Marsh to score a try just before half-time. A spirited Hunslet side were beaten at home thanks to a determined late try from an unstoppable Martin Moana. Defeat followed at Oldham in spite of a monumental display from Lee Marsh who did not deserve to be on the losing team scoring two tries and three goals. A fine victory over Workington at home wrapped up the league campaign with two tries each for Andy Saywell, Martin Moana and Marlon Billy. It was a stirring end-of-season charge that allowed the Lions to reach the play-offs once again. The consequence of the six-point deduction meant the Lions travelled to Oldham instead of Workington in the play-offs.

It will never be known if the Lions would have won at Workington; as it was the Lions were well beaten at Oldham in the Elimination play-off. The Roughyeds hit Swinton hard straight from the kick-off at Boundary Park with mid-season signing Byron Ford from Hull KR proving to be an impressive impact player. The game featured in an episode of the television programme *Rugby League Raw* and footage showed the Swinton dressing room was a very disappointed place after the game as Paul Kidd tried to lift his players. Oldham coach Steve Deakin had assembled a very useful effective side. For the record, Oldham beat

Workington in the next round and then reached the Grand Final after a win at Barrow. Featherstone Rovers eventually won the final at Headingley.

As for the Lions, Paul Kidd was left to consider a few issues not least the reason for the inconsistency of the team. Phil Wood deservedly swept the board in the club's end of season presentation evening and Andy Saywell topped the try-scoring chart with an impressive 21 from 22 appearances, ably supported on the other wing by Marlon Billy. Lee Marsh was the leading point scorer and Wayne English made the most appearances with 28 in all.

2008: The Testimonial season

As the Testimonial season for Wayne English was announced, there were more changes on the playing front which did not help the continuity of the team, especially in preparation for the new season. Several players went to Rochdale Hornets including Paul Alcock, Mark Brocklehurst, Chris Hough, Craig Farrimond and Dave Newton with new recruits joining including Rob Ball, Darren Bamford, Adam Bibey, Darren Gibson, Richie Hawkyard, Gary Hulse and Neil Rigby. The Lions team in 2008 did not fulfil its potential, in spite of these signings, but there is no doubt that an injury crisis as bad as the club has known in living memory caused severe problems. Seasoned professionals such as Chris Morley and Phil Wood, as well as promising youngsters such as Barry Hamilton and Chris Tyrer, all suffered horrific long-term injuries and these problems blighted the entire campaign. Even Wayne sustained a broken jaw which caused him to miss nine games on the trot for the first time in his Swinton career. At one point mid-season, Paul Kidd had only 17 fit players to select from, resulting in the signing of several loan players at various stages such as Paul Rafferty from Barrow and Dane Donoghue from Widnes.

The campaign began with two pre-season friendly fixtures, at Whitehaven and at home to a St Helens XIII. The competitive matches in the Northern Rail Cup began encouragingly with two very close defeats at Oldham and at home to Rochdale Hornets, both by only two points. The next match saw the much anticipated clash at Park Lane with Salford following their relegation from Super League the previous season. After a keenly fought first half, the Lions were still in the game until the hour mark when the visitors cut away to gain a flattering 48–8 victory. Two well-taken tries by Andy Saywell were the highlight for the Swinton fans with the score at 18–8 early in the second period. Park Lane witnessed its highest ever gate for a Swinton game with 1,664 spectators, a decent crowd by any standard. At this time chairman John Kidd confirmed that the club was working hard on the Agecroft site with the view to redeveloping the site as a stadium similar to the work of the M27 Stadium Community Project formed by the Supporters' Trust.

A good win at Rochdale late on in the game gave the Swinton faithful hope ahead of the clash at the Willows against Salford on a Friday evening. In a strange night in so many aspects the Lions went down to a 70–6 defeat. Although some weak tackling did not help the cause against full-time opposition benefiting from Super League parachute payments, the Swinton fans felt there were some dubious refereeing decisions against the Lions. For most Swinton supporters standing behind the posts at the former Willows cricket club end of the ground, some of these decisions were not fully apparent until the following week when they watched highlights of the game on television during the Channel M Rugby League programme *Code XIII*. The other unusual aspect of this match was the attendance. Salford reported that 6,042 spectators watched the game. This figure is almost as big as the crowd that saw the epic encounter in the 1981 John Player Trophy tie in which Swinton triumphed 6–0 when 6,728 attended the memorable encounter.

A hard-earned victory at the Recreation Ground, Whitehaven against amateurs Wath Brow Hornets, where former player and coach Bill Holliday began his rugby league career, was followed by a defeat at home to Oldham in the final Northern Rail Cup game of the season which gave a final disappointing tally of one win in six games in that competition. However, there was terrible news to follow when the untimely death of Alan Buckley was announced in March 2008. Alan was a stalwart of the wonderfully entertaining Swinton side of the 1960s that won back-to-back championships at Station Road. He played seven times for Great Britain between 1963 and 1966 and in later years was the honorary president of the Swinton Lions Supporters' Trust. Alan was a true Swinton legend and his sad passing was a huge loss to his family, his many friends in rugby league and the club he played for with such great distinction.

The league season began with an unconvincing win at Park Lane against an improving Blackpool Panthers side under new coach Martin Crompton and the game began with one minute silence as a mark of deepest respect for Alan Buckley. The match-day programme included many poignant tributes from officials, former players and supporters of the club that all had the genuine privilege of knowing a true rugby league legend. Also, there were glowing testimonies from opponents such as Wigan's Billy Boston and St Helens' Alex Murphy confirming Alan's world-class status.

In terms of the league campaign, the Lions inability to play for the full 80 minutes was demonstrated in the next two away games. The Lions dominated the first half at Keighley only to concede two tries just before half-time giving the home team a platform to build upon in the second period. Some woeful tackling in the first half hour gave Doncaster a commanding 30–0 lead the following week in the Lions' first visit to the impressive Keepmoat Stadium. Then there followed a great fight back against a team coached by Ellery Hanley that culminated in three tries and several near misses before a late Doncaster try denied the Lions even a bonus point. After two tough games in Yorkshire, which saw some creative rugby and no small endeavour nevertheless, both performances, were undermined by inconsistent play that meant only one league point was gained when more were in reach.

In April, the Lions held a gala dinner at Sachas Hotel in Manchester to celebrate the 80th anniversary of the club winning five trophies in one season. The historic achievement has never been repeated and the Swinton club was represented in those days by international players such as Bryn Evans, Martin Hodgson and Billo Rees. All the five cups were together again and covered in blue and white ribbons once more. Pride of place at the event was 100-year old Phyllis Bower, a native of Swinton and Lions supporter now living in Bath, who is the daughter of former Lions director John Charles Robinson. Also present was the son and grandson of Martin Hodgson, who is now rightly installed in the Rugby League Hall of Fame.

Swinton lost again to Oldham in the fourth round of the Challenge Cup either side of wins against London Scholars at Park Lane and a rare away victory against Workington Town, but the latter game proved costly in terms of injuries. In particular, Dean Gorton broke his thumb and wrist while Wayne English suffered a broken jaw in the same game when making a brave tackle on a Town forward who fell awkwardly and accidentally on the Swinton full-back. In Wayne's absence the Lions lost seven out of nine games.

There followed a four game losing run including a defeat at home to Gateshead in which Chris Frodsham, son of former Swinton and St Helens star Tommy, made a try-scoring debut; and a last-minute defeat on the Fylde coast to Blackpool in a game the Lions dominated throughout. The injuries were taking a heavy toll on performance as well as affecting the players' confidence. Victories at Hunslet and a home win over Workington Town to complete a rare double were the only highlights as the miserable weather during the British summer reflected the down beat mood in the Swinton camp. This depressing situation was compounded by another two long-term injuries. First, young prop Chris Tyrer, signed from St Helens Academy at the start of the season, broke his leg and fractured his ankle in a game at home to Rochdale Hornets. Then, inspirational hooker Phil Wood was ruled out for the rest of the season with a suspected dislocated collarbone in the confidence sapping defeat away to London Skolars after new recruit Dave York, a forward from South Africa had been dismissed needlessly for the use of an elbow. Coach Paul Kidd summed-up events when he said: "The [Phil] Wood injury is a massive blow and couldn't come at worse time."

"Wayne English with ball" by John Prince (2008)

Swinton Lions RLFC squad 2007

Wayne English attempts to break through the Blackpool defence 15 May 2005

Wayne English sprints clear of the London Skolars defence 13 April 2008

The return of Wayne and the signing of Mike Wainwright from Leigh, Paul Crook from Doncaster and David Bates after a playing stint in France, lifted the Lions performances but unfortunately not the results as even a bonus point eluded the team. In the second half of the league campaign, the Lions won only once, at home to Hunslet, a result which meant that the South Leeds team finished bottom rather than the Lions who finished third from bottom also ahead of London Skolars. However, the Lions missed a play-off spot by some distance. There were some good-spirited performances in the last two home defeats against high-flying Oldham and Barrow, but this could not mask the end of a very disappointing season. The final game of the season marked the last game in Swinton colours for former Warrington Academy player Chris Hull who having shown glimpses of good ability was scheduled to move to Australia soon after the game.

Altogether, the bright spots of the season included Wayne English's testimonial, Marlon Billy's impressive haul of 17 tries from 22 games, Rickie Hawkyard's kicking game and the debut season of Neil Rigby who won the Alan Buckley Memorial Award for his consistent efforts all season. However, the entire season was blighted by horrendous, long-term injuries to key players and squad members alike. Without making excuses, it is acknowledged that injuries are a part of modern sport, but any club like Swinton with limited resources cannot cope with prolonged absences in a finite pool of players. How different it was for the club 80 years ago when the Lions won five trophies in a single season.

In the weeks that followed the end of the season there was feverish speculation about the future of the club including claims that the team would play the following season at Darwen FC's Anchor Road ground where both John and Paul Kidd are directors. These claims gained validity when it was revealed that Kevin Henry, the chairman at Darwen FC, is also a director at Swinton which added to a general sense of uncertainty. However, in November the club confirmed that it would play the 2009 and 2010 seasons at Park Lane and this ended the immediate speculation. This good news was further augmented by the signing of Halifax-born Graham Holdroyd, the return of local player Paul Southern and former player Danny Heaton all from the Halifax club as well as the announcement by the Trust that Les Holliday would be the new honorary president. Although the club did lose the valuable services of community development manager, John Thomason, who left to do a similar role at Barrow after sterling work locally; the highlight of which had seen him introduce street rugby to parts of Swinton including the Valley Estate.

This brings the story of the Lions up to date and incorporates a very interesting period for the club. It can also be recorded that the celebrity culture has even been apparent with former Swinton player Kris Smith linked romantically with "X Factor" judge and Australian pop diva Dannii Minogue. The relationship has even been featured heavily in gossip magazines and newspapers such as *The News of the World*. As Dave Hadfield commented wryly in the October 2008 edition of *Rugby League World*, Kris Smith never generated so many column inches when playing for Swinton. In fact, Kris spent the vast majority of his playing career with the Lions having played previously for Super League clubs such as Halifax and London Broncos before finishing his career with 10 games at Oldham in 2007. In terms of rugby league, Kris has continued his involvement in the game and was recently appointed the assistant coach at the local amateur Eccles club.

Finally, the Lions were featured in *The Observer* in October in an article lamenting the demise of the much-loved Station Road ground. The article provided timely evidence that the Lions deserve a new stadium back in the boundaries of Swinton and Pendlebury. The dream could one day become a reality now the team is training at the Agecroft site under temporary floodlights paid for in part by the Supporters Trust. As for Wayne, he was still training hard and enjoyed his Testimonial season with the Lions.

4. The future and reflections on a professional

"In the semi-professional world of National League football it is a rarity to see such long-term loyalty today, and it is truly a credit to Wayne that he has remained at the Lions for ten years."
Paul Kidd (2008) writing about Wayne English

Introduction

The opinion from the changing room about Wayne English confirms a consensus that he is a hugely likeable character off the pitch but tough on it. The players at Swinton have benefited from Wayne's consistent performances and the coaches have clearly appreciated his honest style of play which is why he has been selected over 200 times for Swinton. Also, the backroom staff and officials have a wealth of Wayne-related anecdotes to add to the general stock of Swinton stories passed-on over the years. From his error against Dewsbury to his faultless display in the Grand Final against Sheffield Eagles, Wayne has provided many memorable moments. While the career of Wayne English is not over, nevertheless this is an ideal opportunity to reflect and also look to the future using the testimonies of his fellow professionals, coaches, officials and backroom staff at Swinton.

The players

Marlon Billy was in the Swinton side on the wing when Wayne made his debut in 2000 and he has appeared on the Swinton team-sheet along side Wayne more than any other player. Marlon's first impression of Wayne on the night he made his first appearance in a Swinton shirt was that he was too small and Marlon was concerned he would get hurt. However, he soon discovered that Wayne is a strong unit who can look after himself and cover-tackle to great effect. Wayne is also very effective at returning the ball from a kick according to Marlon and this ability makes life better for any winger. For this reason Marlon has nick-named Wayne the "legend" and jokes with him about who is the toughest player from Rochdale.

Huddersfield-born Marlon has made 155 appearances for Swinton including five as substitute, scoring 84 tries in two spells from 1999 to 2000 and from 2005 to date. Marlon is loyal to the Lions and is grateful to Les Holliday for signing him from Keighley for his first spell at the club. As a winger Marlon is in a good position to comment on Wayne as a player since the full-back and the two wingers form the back three in a rugby league team. He is amazed by Wayne's lightening pace and "magic feet" and notes that sometimes even Wayne doesn't know what he is going to do next. However, Marlon believes that Wayne's unpredictability as a ball-carrier is an asset and whilst it is sometimes difficult to support Wayne when he's in possession of the ball nevertheless he can "dummy" most opponents to create an opening making him a dangerous opponent to face and wonderful to play along side.

Peter Cannon is a good friend of Wayne who featured prominently in the Swinton team when Wayne was establishing himself as a first-team regular and an automatic choice in the full-back position. In two spells at Swinton from 1995 to 1998 and from 2002 to 2004 he made 134 appearances for Swinton including 19 as substitute, scoring 39 tries. As far as Peter is concerned, Wayne is unlike the typical rugby league player. Wayne is neither big in size nor a big talker. Before games, Wayne rarely says much in the changing rooms and has his own quiet way of preparing. On the field of play, Peter was always impressed with Wayne's ability to read play and then often beat the first tackler when carrying the ball forward. This knack resulted in many counter-attacking opportunities for the team.

Off the field of play, it is clear that Wayne does not dwell on performances for days on end and this approach may account for his longevity in the game. Of course, Wayne wants to win but relaxing after the game is important as well which is why he has a good rapport with the Swinton supporters. Peter would joke with team-mates that Wayne bears a strong resemblance to Paddy McGuinness; a Bolton comedian who appeared in Peter Kay's acclaimed television comedy *Phoenix Nights*. While this is pure banter, Peter's assessment that Wayne English is as good a full-back as Mark Welsby is genuine praise from someone who has played along-side both players.

Jason Roach had a phenomenal try-scoring record at Swinton during three spells at the club from 1995 to 1996, in 2000 and from 2002 to 2004. Jason also played Super League for Castleford and Warrington in between spells at the Lions before ending his playing career at Barrow and Blackpool Panthers. His first impression of Wayne was whether this slight young lad would be big enough, but any doubts were soon dispelled by the elusive nature of his play. Jason regards Wayne's approach as part of entertaining the crowd especially when the modern way in rugby league tends to be based on keeping possession. Wayne will always try to make breaks and create opportunities even if that means he will spill the ball on occasion or sometimes be tackled into touch.

Jason also makes an interesting comparison regarding Wayne. When Jason began his professional rugby league career in the St Helens Academy he encountered a young full-back named Steve Prescott and at the time many in the game questioned whether Steve was big enough to endure all the hard knocks. In fact, Steve went on to make 154 Super League appearances for Saints, Hull and Wakefield. When Jason returned to Swinton in 2000 he was reminded of Steve when he met the young Wayne English. Both are full-backs, but neither player is big and yet both players have tremendous strength and great ability in defence and attack.

When Wayne made his return from injury in July 2008 in an evening kick-off at home to Doncaster, the Sedgley Park first team were training using weights by the side of the clubhouse at the same time. One of the Sedgley Park players was Andy Craig who had switched to rugby union after a successful rugby league career including a couple of spells at Swinton. In a strange coincidence, he was in the Swinton team when Wayne made his debut in 2000. He watched the game for short while and asked why on earth Wayne was playing on the wing. The decision was not at all clear, but given that Wayne was returning from a serious injury it can be assumed that Paul Kidd was easing him back into the first-team given there was no reserve team set-up. In fact, Gary Hulse had played at full-back in Wayne's absence and had delivered some good performances. Normal service was resumed for the final six games of the campaign as Wayne regained the full-back berth.

It is interesting to note that whilst Wayne has remained at a single club Andy Craig left for new challenges including playing in the rival code. At the start of his career, Andy who is originally from St Helens, played 10 times in Super League for Wigan in the 1996 season scoring two tries. He is mentioned in Martin Offiah's autobiography, first published in 1997, when they met one another in Warrington during the weekend Offiah played rugby league for London Broncos and rugby union for Bedford. By this time Andy was in his first spell at Swinton before he left to play Supper League again in 1999 this time at Halifax where he played 20 times scoring a single try and three goals. He was back at Swinton in 2000 teaming up with Mike Gregory who was also the Scotland Rugby League assistant coach at the time and played 26 times scoring 16 tries before moving away once more this time to play rugby union in the winter for Orrell. By 2002, Andy was representing Scotland at rugby union having played previously for Scotland at rugby league in 1999. He became the first former Swinton player to make this journey from the XIII-a-side game to the XV-a-side at international level. In all, he was capped twice in league and 13 times in union mostly in his favoured position of centre against teams as varied as England, Wales, South Africa, Canada, Romania and Fiji scoring a hat-trick against the latter at Murrayfield.

Strangely, Andy Craig was not the first English–born centre three-quarter with Swinton connections to represent Scotland at rugby union. In 1889, James Marsh who played for Swinton and Edinburgh Institution when studying to be a doctor in the Scottish capital was capped twice by Scotland even though he was an Englishman. Three years later he was capped again this time by England in spite of fierce Scottish objections also in the centre position against Ireland one of the teams he played against for Scotland.

The coaches

Brent Andrews coached the young Wayne English and has always kept an eye on the Swinton team-sheet to see if Wayne has been selected to play. So much so, that he knew there was a problem straight after Wayne suffered a jaw injury at Workington in 2008 as his name was no longer appearing in the Swinton line-up. Brent has seen Wayne play professionally several times, usually when the Lions are playing Rochdale Hornets at Spotland. He recognises straight away the distinctive style of play and electric pace which he first saw in the 10 year old Wayne English. Brent was one of the first players when Kirkholt WMC formed a rugby league section which is where Wayne went to play his amateur rugby league. Brent now coaches at Rochdale Mayfield in the junior section and often sees Wayne around Rochdale, but knows that he is too modest to elaborate on his career in any detail. In this sense, Wayne is like many other rugby league players who are content to play the game and be part of a team at whatever level. Wayne's success does not surprise Brent who knows the "first to training" attitude is an essential requirement in the tough world of professional sport and especially rugby league.

Wayne has been coached at Swinton by a number of influential figures. When Wayne arrived first at Gigg Lane, the legendary Les Holliday was head coach. Les is the son of Great Britain international Bill Holliday who played for Whitehaven, Hull KR, Swinton and Rochdale Hornets in the 1960s and early 1970s. Bill joined Swinton in 1968 for a club record fee of £6,000 and settled in the area after retiring from playing. This meant that his two gifted sons; Les and Mike played amateur rugby league for Swinton's local team Folly Lane ARLFC. As a result, Les signed for the Lions in 1982 and never looked back. He captained the Lions in the 1987 Second Division Premiership final at Old Trafford playing along side his younger brother Mike. Les eventually moved to Halifax playing in a Challenge Cup Final at Wembley in 1988 before signing for Widnes. Then he signed for Dewsbury and finally back to Swinton on 4 August 1995, but not before he was capped for Great Britain like his father. During his time as Swinton coach, Les kept a watching brief on the academy team coached by John Prince that included Wayne English. Les was head coach from March 1997 to May 1999 when he was replaced by assistant coach Mike Gregory who had been previously assistant coach at St Helens.

Mike Gregory, the Wigan-born former Warrington second row forward who played 20 times for Great Britain between 1987 and 1990, is the Swinton coach who gave Wayne his first team debut. Having replaced Les Holliday as first team coach, Mike spent another two full seasons in charge. Gregory was a huge influence on Wayne and a coach who inspired confidence in his players. However, at the end of a disappointing 2001 season, Mike Gregory's contract was not renewed by chairman Malcolm White who explained he needed a coach with more contacts in the amateur game. As the part-time England academy coach, Gregory was more associated with elite full-time Rugby League players at the top clubs including Gareth Hock, Luke Robinson and Jon Wilkin. Also, in the England Academy squad at the time was Bruce Johnson who signed subsequently for the Lions in 2006 and became an instant success.

Tony Humphries was in charge briefly at Gigg Lane in 2002 with Mark Sheals as assistant coach. Tony signed for the club as a player on 25 March 1993 having been previously at Warrington and Rochdale Hornets. In total, Tony played 81 times for Swinton including six substitute appearances and scored eight tries from the combative prop position in the front-row of the pack. Tony was a good communicator and well liked initially as coach, but Wayne's chances in the first-team were restricted at this time. However, following a disastrous start to the 2002 season when the Lions had won only one of the first eleven games and that was against Hull amateurs Skirlaugh in the Challenge Cup, he was replaced by Australian Phil Veivers, the first antipodean in charge at Swinton since Chris O'Sullivan in 1992 when the Lions were in the old First Division.

Incidentally, along-side Sullivan in that last season at Station Road was compatriot Craig Bellamy who went onto fabulous success as head coach at Melbourne Storm, taking charge in 2003. In October 2008, the Melbourne Storm club had reached the Australian NRL Grand Final for the third year in a row. Bellamy also coaches the New South Wales State of Origin team, which is quite an achievement for a former Swinton player.

Former Saints star Phil Veivers took over the coaching role part way through the troubled 2002 season after Tony Barrow had been caretaker coach. Veivers signed originally for St Helens in September 1984 and had enjoyed an illustrious career at full-back. He finished his playing career with the Lions in 2001 scoring 5 tries in 21 appearances including one as substitute playing mainly at loose-forward. Veivers used his vast experience and leadership qualities on and off the pitch at Swinton to great effect and was able to impart some of his knowledge of the game to the younger Swinton players such as Wayne English who played the same full-back role that Veivers played with such distinction at Knowsley Road. However, Swinton could not keep hold of such a talented coach and eventually Veivers left by the end of the 2002 season.

Peter Roe first arrived at Swinton in January 1996 and stayed until March 1997. When he arrived back as coach at the start of the 2003 season, the Lions were based at Moor Lane. It is Peter who was the first Swinton coach to consistently select Wayne English at full-back. This is not surprising because as early as 2000, Roe was quick to note the talents of Wayne English when he was coach of Featherstone Rovers. Roe is a formidable character and someone the players respect enormously. In turn, Roe rewards consistent performers, which is why Wayne was selected for every game in 2003 (except when serving a two-game suspension). Also, Roe noticed the loyalty of Wayne and is once quoted as saying: "Wayne has blue and white blood running through his veins." This is high praise indeed from a respected rugby league coach.

Paul Kidd is the Swinton coach who has the distinction of coaching Wayne for the longest period of time. Paul has served the club in many capacities and from 2004, he became head coach initially with Les Holliday as director of rugby and this coaching partnership steered the Lions to the 2006 Grand Final. Paul is in no doubt about Wayne's contribution to the Lions. He views his loyalty through the highs and lows as truly remarkable and notes this is rare in the semi-professional reaches of the game outside Super League.

The officials
Tony Barrow senior was the chief executive at Swinton in the period around the millennium and was a former coach from January 1992 to January 1996 joining as successor to Chris O'Sullivan when the club had a few months left at Station Road. Tony was a successful centre for St Helens in the 1960s and coached Warrington and Oldham before joining Swinton. He was an influential figure at the club for over 10 years before leaving in October 2002 just after the move to Moor Lane. Tony fulfilled many roles at Swinton in the decade he was associated with the club. He was instrumental in bringing John Prince to the club when the successful Academy set-up was established in the 1990s. As a result, Tony was there at the start of several successful professional careers that began at Swinton including Andy Coley, Phil Cushion, Mick Nanyn, Paul Smith and of course Wayne English.

An intriguing insight into the career of Wayne English is provided by former Swinton Director Richard Taylor and lifelong Swinton supporter, who also chaired Wayne's Testimonial Committee. Richard recalls that Mike Gregory would have liked to have taken Wayne to Wigan as understudy to Kris Radlinski after the 2003 Challenge Cup Quarter-final; and that Brian Noble also made enquires about Wayne when he was head coach at Bradford Bulls although no formal offer was made on either occasion. However, the bigger clubs were taking note of Wayne's performances and it was only a matter of time before an actual offer materialised.

The three definite offers that did arrive to take Wayne away from Swinton were received around 2003 as the rugby league world began to notice the talented full-back. First, Widnes made an offer that would have given Wayne significantly extra money, but a prolonged spell in the reserves so the deal was rejected. Secondly, Sheffield Eagles tried to tempt Wayne with an offer, but the extra travelling to South Yorkshire eventually ruled out the deal. Finally and most significantly, Castleford made a cash offer of £4,000 to Swinton plus a signing-on fee of about £12,000 for Wayne. This deal was very tempting and Wayne accepted provisionally (and reluctantly) in spite of few people knowing the details. In what would have been Wayne's last game as a Swinton player, he was pensive before kick-off, understandably with his mind on the transfer and not the game. As he ran onto the Moor Lane pitch, he saw a home-made banner which read "Wayne don't go" draped along the opposite touchline. Subsequently, he played a below par game by his high standards and went straight to the club's directors afterwards and told them that the deal was off. Wayne has remained at Swinton ever since. No one but Wayne knows whether this incident changed his mind alone, but one thing is for certain he did not stay at Swinton for the money. He remained at Swinton because he is loyal to the club and its supporters.

It is possible any of these potential moves could have made Wayne a better player or a lot of money and possibly even both. The only significant criticism about Wayne as a player centres on his passing ability. He can pass the ball well; and at training he is as good as the best of the other players. Not quite at the standard of Andy Gregory in his prime, but no modern day rugby league player can match the way he sent the ball spinning into the hands of a team-mate with a perfectly timed pass that unlocked the best defences in the world. Richard Taylor recalls that Mike Gregory observed Wayne tended to hold the ball as a counter-weight rather than in readiness to pass. If true, this explains how Wayne can somersault literally through tackles but consequently makes him less able to get a pass out. Given that Wayne plays at full-back and not at half-back then perhaps this is not a massive issue in any case.

Richard Taylor concludes that Wayne English is more deserving of a Testimonial than most players in Super League since the level at which Wayne plays the game part-time is raw with limited off-the-field resources. The mark of a true sportsman is any one who plays even though the rewards are not great and when a terrible injury is a badly-timed tackle away.

The backroom staff
Norman Brown is the long-serving physio at Swinton who has not missed a training session at the club let alone a first team game since the mid-1970s. What Norman doesn't know about Swinton is probably not worth knowing. He has seen every player at close quarter and he could write an entire book about his reminiscences given the many things he's witnessed down the years. Norman regards Wayne as a very honest player who has avoided his share of serious injuries through being tough. Colin Robinson, who is also part of the

backroom staff at Swinton and a former physio, shares this assessment of Wayne English.

Vinny Kirkman is the kit-man at Swinton having been for many years also known as "Vinny the Lion", a Lion mascot par excellence. It was while in the lion suit that Vinny first met the young Wayne English although the exact occasion has been lost to posterity. Vinny has a great deal of time for Wayne and admires what he has done for the club. He knows that the club would have struggled without Wayne over the past decade. Even so, Vinny recalls the time when Wayne missed the team coach on the way to a friendly fixture at Whitehaven early in 2008. Paul Kidd told Wayne on his mobile telephone to make his own way from Rochdale to Forton Service Station on the M6 where there was a scheduled stop for the team to have a light pre-match meal. A while later Wayne calls back asking how far Forton is past the Huddersfield junction on the M62. Unfortunately, it transpired he was heading east-bound in an altogether different direction. Wayne did have the last laugh though. The coach transporting the Swinton team actually broke down soon after and when Wayne arrived at Whitehaven just before 3 o'clock he did so before any other of the Swinton players and officials on the coach. The delayed kick-off gave Wayne the chance to recover from his long (and detoured) journey.

Of course, John Prince was the person who brought Wayne to Swinton in the first place. He describes Wayne as a "Jack Russell" type of player who is compact, but consistent in the way he approaches the game. Although John's untimely accident early in Wayne's professional career prevented him from even greater involvement with the Lions, nevertheless John had already paved the way for Wayne to be a raising star in the blue and white colours of Swinton. For that contribution alone every Swinton supporter will be eternally grateful to John Prince.

The future
Wayne is relatively young to be granted a testimonial. The previous Swinton player to be granted a testimonial was Alex Melling in 1993 who became 30 years of age that season. Melling was a stalwart of the Swinton pack for many years during a period that covered the end of the Station Road era and the start of playing at Gigg Lane. He is now the chairman of Oldham St Anne's ARLFC and active in amateur rugby league in the Oldham area.

As for Wayne, he is keen to continue playing for as long as he can, which he hopes will be with Swinton. No-one knows what the future holds, but Wayne has declared on several occasions that he wants to be a Swinton player when he receives a second testimonial in 2018. This is a feat achieved only once before at Swinton by Ken Gowers although Jim Valentine served the club well for almost two decades in the late Victorian era. Incidentally, Ken Gowers was a goalkicking full-back like his father Walter Gowers who starred for Rochdale Hornets and both toured Australia and New Zealand with Great Britain; Walter in 1928 and Ken in 1966. Wayne has never kicked at goal instead leaving this specialist role to others in the Swinton team. Interestingly, Wayne has probably rarely kicked the ball during the game in spite being a goalkicker in his amateur days. Of course, given his pace and agility he has never really needed to kick the ball, either.

It is clear that Wayne is a decent, honest player and fair with his fellow professionals. He has only once been sent off in his professional career (at London Skolars) and occasions when Wayne loses his cool are very rare indeed. One such episode happened in a league game in 2003 at Chorley's Victory Park against a talented team coached by Darren Abram. In a relatively tight contest, Wayne scored a try to close the gap to nine points with just seven minutes remaining. What allegedly happened next was unusual for Wayne. As wingman Chris Campbell crossed for the decisive Chorley try Wayne appeared to take a "head-shot" at the player who apparently retaliated. Wayne was put on report for the incident with the offence of a 'high tackle' cited as the reason. Trevor Baxter, reporting for the *Rugby Leaguer and League Express*, described Wayne as "fiery" for probably the first and only time in Wayne's career and commented that he was lucky not to be dismissed. Whether it was the close nature of the game, the local derby element, disappointment at losing the game or the fact that the Chorley's team contained a number of former Lions (and two future Lions) there is no doubt that Wayne was indeed very close to being sent-off again. What happens at close quarters in a rugby league game is a series of fierce contests in which individual players attempt to control the game for the overall benefit of the team. It is not a game for the faint-hearted, but certainly Wayne has improved his discipline over the years to a level where he never even questions a refereeing decision never mind throws a punch at an opponent or gets into an altercation.

Wayne also has ambitions as a coach in the future. He has already coached the Whitworth ARLFC under-12s junior team and enjoyed the experience back in the amateur game. Whitworth is located three miles north of Rochdale and the area had a fledgling professional rugby league team based at Tong Lane around the beginning of the twentieth century. As for Wayne, rugby league has been his life since he was nine years old and he is committed to staying in the game for a long time. Whatever the outcome, Wayne has a young family and he sees his daughter Alicia as his long-term priority. For the record, Wayne and Nina got married in February 2009.

So in 2009, the Swinton club has an ideal opportunity to shape its own future. While there has been much speculation about a potential move to Darwen the club is set to remain at Sedgley Park for the next two seasons. What happens after this time is far from certain but a move to a new purpose-built stadium in Swinton and Pendlebury at Agecroft for example would be the ideal way for Wayne English to finish his playing career at the Lions.

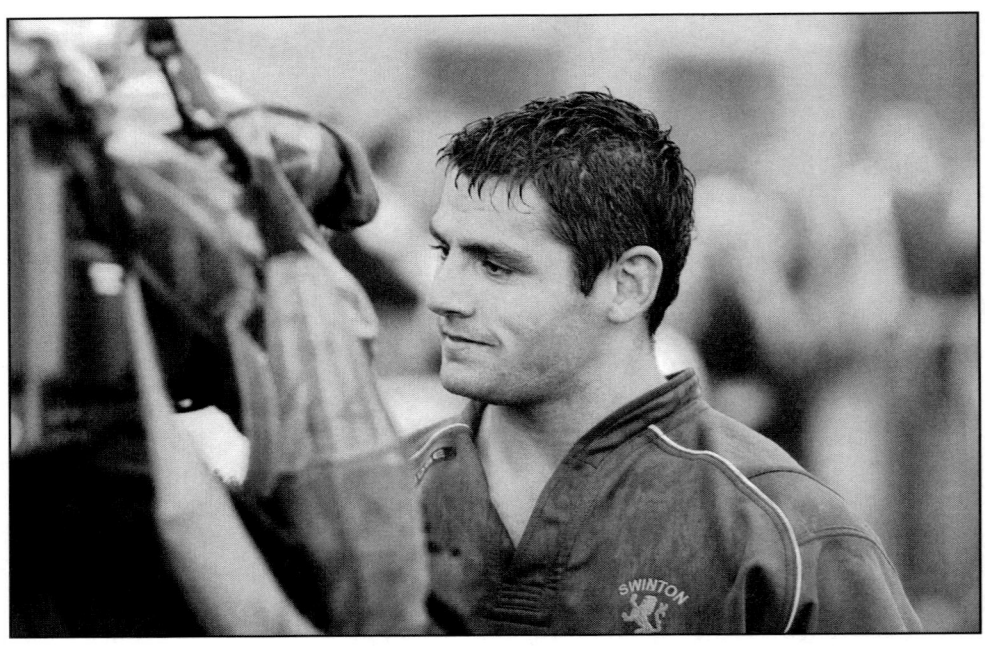

Post-match interview:
Wayne contemplates victory over Celtic Crusaders at Brewery Field, 1 October 2006

5. Swinton full-backs since 1866

Wayne English is the latest Swinton full-back to serve the club well. Over the years there have been some outstanding players in this key position for the Lions. The following potted history covers some of the finest full-backs for Swinton since formation in 1866. Many of the players gained international caps and have been honoured to tour Australia and New Zealand while others played their part in securing silverware for the club. All have worn the number one shirt in the blue and white colours of Swinton with great distinction and each one has provided great entertainment for the supporters.

Swinton Football Club was formed by cricketers in the town at a meeting at St Peter's Church in October 1866 as a way of keeping fit during the winter months. The original games were played on a field close to Station Road and those taking part were restricted to club members. In January 1869, the first properly competitive match took place against the (Swinton and Eccles) Number One Company of the 46th Lancashire Rifle Volunteers. The game was seven-a-side and best described as a hybrid form of football so there was probably no recognisable full-back position as such. The adoption of organised rules arrived in 1871 when the club joined the Rugby Football Union in the first year of its formation.

One of the very first Swinton full-backs to excel was **Tom Farr** who also played in the threequarter line. Tom was an outstanding sportsman from this early period and opened the batting for Swinton Cricket Club. Indeed, at the time the cricket club was regarded as the senior of the two organisations which is why the rugby season was restricted to the months between October and March to allow Tom Farr and others such as John Dorning and Joe Mills to participate in both sports. Tom was the son of a local physician and one of four brothers who played for Swinton; the others being Herbert, Edward and Henry. Tom Farr played in the historic first meeting between Swinton and Manchester hosted at Manchester's international ground at Whalley Range on 16 March 1878 witnessed a by huge crowd of 4,500 spectators. In those days, teams played with two full-backs and Tom partnered his brother Edward as the Lions triumphed against a Manchester side full of international players including Albert Neilson 'Monkey' Hornby, the dual England cricket and rugby captain. This result catapulted the Swinton club to national fame and by the end of the season they were undefeated for the third successive year with Tom kicking seven goals; the most for the club that season. Eventually, Tom went onto to represent Lancashire five times at rugby union between 1882 and 1884 scoring four tries. He was also captain for the Lions in the 1879–80 and 1883–84 seasons.

Sam Roberts was another outstanding player in this pioneering era and can claim to be recognised as one of the best full-backs in the entire country at the time. Sam, originally from Bury, was selected to play for England in 1887, which was a huge achievement and he became only the third Swinton player to receive such an honour following Ted Beswick in 1882 and Charlie Horley in 1885. In all, Sam gained two England caps by which time rugby teams had settled on one player in the full-back position. The first cap for Sam was a scoreless draw at Stradey Park, Llanelli against Wales on 8 January 1887; and the second was a defeat to Ireland at Landsdowne Road, Dublin on 5 February. Many of the England players in the team were from Blackheath and Richmond, but others were from northern gate-taking clubs such as Dewsbury (Dickie Lockwood) and Broughton Rangers (Robert Seddon). The following season, Robert Seddon joined Swinton and subsequently captained the first-ever touring side from Great Britain to Australia and New Zealand in 1888 but drowned tragically part way through the tour in the Hunter River near Maitland, New South Wales. As for Sam, he also represented the North in the 1886–87 season and played seven times for Lancashire between 1886 and 1889 scoring seven goals in total. Sam had a lasting impression on the Swinton club and in 1927 he was featured on a programme cover under the title: "Sam Roberts: a clean sportsman who played the game".

At around the same time was another outstanding Swinton full-back **Arthur Paul**, who had a unique sporting profile. Arthur was not typical of Swinton players at the time since he was a trained architect and cricket professional. He was born in Belfast, the son of an Army Colonel and was described as tall and robust by the *Wisden Cricket Almanack* and also as a batsman of high skill. As well as playing for Swinton and Lancashire at rugby union, Arthur Paul also went to Australia and New Zealand with the first-ever rugby tour from Britain along with fellow Swinton players Walter Bumby, Tom Banks and the ill-fated Robert Seddon. While on tour, there were games of Australian Rules Football in the state of Victoria by which time England cricket and rugby international Andrew Stoddart had taken over as tour captain. After the tour, Paul played as a first-class cricketer in the summer for Lancashire from 1889 to 1900 after qualifying to play for the county with Nelson Cricket Club. He made his highest score of 177 at Taunton in 1895 in partnership with Archie MacLaren who made a first-class record of 424 runs. In a remarkable sporting career, he also played as a goalkeeper for Blackburn Rovers in 1899. After retiring from all sporting endeavours due to ill-health, Arthur was invited to coach county cricket at Lancashire and he was eventually awarded a benefit at Old Trafford in 1913 with the Lancashire committee contributing £400. He died at his home in Didsbury in January 1947 aged 82.

Alf Chorley was the celebrated Swinton full-back in the period after the club switched from rugby union to Northern Union as rugby league was known at the time. His career spanned from 1898 to 1905 and he became the first Swinton player to appear in every single game of the season as a Northern Union club in 1901–02 season. Also, Alf played full-back when Swinton defeated Salford 16–8 at Fallowfield, Manchester in the 1900 Challenge Cup Final. Around this time, it was not unknown for **James Valentine** to play at full-back although he played mainly as a centre. His contribution is worthy of mention, simply by virtue of his monumental achievements at Swinton in a career that spanned both rugby union and the breakaway Northern Union. James was capped four times as an England rugby union international, the fifth and last Swinton player to be awarded this honour. He was captain of the Lions for many seasons and helped the club cement a national reputation as a fine football team. As a result, he is regarded by many as the greatest Swinton player of all time. James was killed tragically by lightning in 1904 while on holiday with his family in Barmouth and is buried at St John's church in Pendlebury.

Matt Ryder was a stalwart for the club playing mainly at full-back before and during the First World War. He started in the centre and found some useful goalkicking form during the 1911–12 season and finished the season with 12 goals plus two tries. Subsequently, he topped the Swinton goal scoring chart with 33 goals (plus 4 tries) in the 1912–13 season; 37 goals (plus 4 tries) in the 1913–14 season and 24 goals (plus 1 try) in the 1914–15 season, although not all from the full-back position. Then the full devastating horrors of Great War arrived and all competitive fixtures were cancelled until 1919. Matt played as often as he could during the war in friendly games as he also served as a gunner in the army. In spite of it all, he was selected to represent the Lancashire League in 1915–16 season. Matt returned finally from active service to play again in the competitive matches after the war and finished a distinguished playing career in the 1921–22 season. It is worth noting that out of the 40 Swinton players who enlisted 13 were killed as the carnage of the Great War took a dreadful toll on the club.

In the period between the world wars, two full-backs served the Lions well namely, **Jack Pearson** and **Bob Scott**. Jack Pearson signed from Height Recreation amateur club and was the son of former Swinton player Billy Pearson. Jack made his debut for the Lions on 31 December 1921 at home to Batley and was ever-present in the 1922–23 season. He later played in the Challenge Cup Final winning team of 1925–26 and played 31 games in the Five Cups season of 1927–28. Jack was a talented player for Swinton and will always be remembered as part of sporting history when the Lions swept all before them in the late 1920s. Bob Scott made his Swinton debut on 8 December 1928 at home to Hunslet having become a free agent following the demise of the short-lived

Carlisle City RLFC. Originally from Aspatria, he played 37 times in the Lions' Championship season of 1930–31 and 34 times in the Championship season of 1934–35, as the Lions dominated the game. Gus Risman described him as "Safe as the Bank of England" and his career lasted 472 games initially for Batley and then Huddersfield before he joined Carlisle City and finally Swinton. Bob also played nine times for Cumberland as a Swinton player and 21 times for his county in total including the epic defeat of the 1933 touring Australians at Whitehaven.

The period after the Second World War proved to be relatively harsh for the fortunes of Swinton especially in comparison to the great teams of the 1920s and 1930s. Nevertheless, immediately after the war, **Ralph Morgan** played at full-back and even earned a call-up into the Wales Rugby League team playing three times between 1948 and 1950 scoring two goals. In the early 1950s, Swinton signed a young player from Wigan named **Albert Blan** who also challenged Ralph for the full-back position. Eventually, Albert moved to the loose-forward position which better suited his craft and guile as he was one of the cleverest footballers ever to wear a Swinton shirt. A decade later he captained Swinton to two successive Rugby League championships.

The great Swinton team of the late 1950s and 1960s had a truly world-class player at full-back. **Ken Gowers** is a legend of the club who played from 1954 to 1973 and gained 14 Great Britain caps. He was vice-captain on the 1966 Lions tour to Australia and New Zealand. Ken made the full-back spot his own following his debut in 1954. In total, Ken amassed 2,105 points in his Swinton career and played 593 times plus 8 appearances as substitute, which are both club records. In the two Championship seasons, he played 27 times in both, namely the 1962–63 and 1963–64 seasons as the Lions dominated the First Division era. Ken must have had a wonderful view as the Swinton three-quarter line of Speed, Fleet, Buckley and Stopford clicked into gear and ripped apart opposing defences. By the end of his career at Swinton, Ken was playing at half-back as often as he was at full-back. Over a 20 year period, Ken was a great presence on and off the field of play. He influenced the young players and the old professionals alike and instilled a winning mentality at the club that stands the test of time. There have been other full-backs of note at Swinton since the halcyons days of the 1960s but Ken Gowers was truly a hard act to follow.

Both Swinton-born **Paul Jackson** and Leigh-born **Stan Gittins** were notable full-backs for the Lions in the 1970s. Paul played at full-back in the last Swinton team to reach a major final when the Lions lost 25–11 against Salford at Warrington in 1972 Lancashire Cup final. Stan was a useful acquisition from Batley and eventually served Swinton well over many years in a coaching capacity. In addition, **Graeme Johns** played well at full-back at a difficult time for the Lions when the glory days of the 1960s were starting to fade and the crowds at Station Road were beginning to diminish.

Wigan-based **John Gorton** initially broke into the Swinton side in the 1976–77 season but took a couple of years to dislodge Graeme Johns from the full-back position. John had trials at Liverpool Football Club and even roomed with Jimmy Case on away trips before switching permanently to rugby league and eventually played and scored in every Swinton game of the 1980–81 season all from the full-back position. He was the first Swinton player to achieve this feat and to date he is the only player to do so. Incidentally, John featured prominently in the opening credits of the acclaimed Yorkshire Television documentary *Another bloody Sunday* about the plight of perennial strugglers Doncaster. He is captured tackling Tony Banham, the huge Doncaster prop, at a time when most Swinton games seemed to be all mud and no glory. Other Swinton players that featured include Tony Cooper, Kel Earl, Alva Drummond and an unknown trialist whose name was later revealed as none other than Danny Wilson.

Kevin O'Loughlin as a former Wigan player added a touch of class when he played at full-back for Swinton. Although his time at Swinton was at the end of his professional career, he still performed to the very high standard that had earned him Great Britain under-24 caps, appearances for Lancashire and rave reviews whilst at Central Park. Kevin signed for his home-town club Wigan from Warrington Colts and between 1963 and 1975 he made 284 appearances scoring 25 tries and 57 goals. During the majority of his time at Wigan, Kevin played for legendary Wigan coach Eric Ashton who honed his rugby league talent to great effect. In particular, Kevin's tackling technique was quite exceptional and his cover defence superb. Kevin began his Swinton career at loose-forward on 21 August 1977 in a heavy defeat at St Helens in the Lancashire Cup. He stayed in that position for most of his first season moving to centre the following year. He made the occasional appearance at full-back in the next couple of seasons and from 1981 to 1983 played in the number one shirt mainly as cover for Paul Mellor. Although Kevin was regarded by many as a utility player, nevertheless his positional sense and great natural talent, schooled over many year at Wigan, allowed him to excel for the Lions at full-back as well as in the centre and at loose-forward.

It is a fact often overlooked that **David Watkins** played for Swinton in the 1979–80 season after his final game for Salford on April fool's day 1979 against Rochdale Hornets. Swinton became only the third club team that Watkins played for following his celebrated move to Salford from Newport RFC. Born at Blaina, Monmouthshire, the son of a coal-miner, David first played in the black and amber hoops of Newport at Rodney Parade before he was capped for Wales and the British Lions as a fly-half. One of his finest games for Newport was the defeat of the New Zealand tourist in 1963 the same year he won his first cap for Wales. A reported fee totalling £16,000 took him to the Willows in October 1967 and he made his debut at home against Oldham. However, he never reached his full potential in the stand-off position in rugby league having excelled in that position in rugby union. He switched to full-back with Salford and also took over the kicking duties and never looked back. David made his Swinton debut at Station Road against Dewsbury on 2 September 1979 as a full-back and in total played 20 times for the Lions scoring two tries, 19 goals and 9 drop-goals. He played full-back, in the centres and also at stand-off and remarked that at Swinton "Playing full-back behind that defence was like playing behind a colander, there were that many holes." After finishing with the Lions he played three more times for the short-lived Cardiff City Blue Dragons RLFC in the 1982–83 season at the age of 40. He is now president of Newport Gwent Dragons and back in the rugby union fold.

Paul Mellor was a fine attacking full-back for Swinton from 1980 onwards who also played for the Great Britain Colts in the 1981–82 season. He scored a try and four goals in his one appearance against France in Limoux and was awarded the man-of-the-match award after Great Britain won 15–4. This is indicative of the talent that Paul possessed as the Lions were in the Second Division at the time. Paul was the product of the local Langworthy ARLFC based in Pendlebury and he followed in the footsteps of his elder brother Johnny when he signed for the Lions at the start of the 1980–81 season. There was no doubting his ability as a free-flowing full-back with a great deal of bravery in defence. However, Paul's very promising early career was ruined by injury and in the end whilst his playing career lasted over 11 seasons he made only 94 appearances scoring 10 tries and 94 goals. To his credit, Paul never gave-up on his Swinton career and made several comebacks, often against the odds, which is why is so fondly remembered by the Swinton supporters who saw him play. Indeed, after a three year gap due to injury he returned in 1989 to make 16 more appearances for the club over the next two seasons. This was dedication to the Swinton cause above and beyond the call of duty. Perhaps his finest match was in the 6–0 victory over Salford at the Willows in the John Player Trophy quarter-final when he and his brother Johnny, who starred in the scrum-half position, played out of their skin, especially in defence and contributed to keeping the opposition scoreless. At heart, Paul is Swinton through and through and he still watches the Lions at Segdley Park.

Andy Rippon arrived at Swinton in the 1984–85 season having signed from Fulham. In that first season he played for Great Britain under-21s as he tried to establish himself in the first team against some tough competition from Paul Mellor amongst other contenders. In five seasons, Andy's first team chances were limited to 65 appearances for the Lions including 19 as substitute in which he scored 6 tries and 104 goals. Andy played for Trafford Borough based at Altrincham's Moss Lane ground after leaving Swinton at the start of the 1989–90 season. About the same time, **Mark Viller** also arrived at the club who played at full-back on occasion although his favoured position was in the centres. Without doubt Mark had his finest game when he played at full-back in the 1987 Second Division Premiership Final against Hunslet at Old Trafford when the Lions won 27–10. Mark was a tough player who never shirked a tackle and was a great asset to the team as a utility player. Mark signed for Rochdale Hornets after he left Swinton.

Paul Topping signed from amateurs Wigan St Patrick's ARLFC and became a consistent performer at Station Road but he owes a great deal of his success to the coaching skills of Jim Crellin. It is obvious that Jim, who is originally from Whitehaven, spotted a great deal of potential in Paul and signed the young Topping on loan from Swinton for six games in the 1986–87 season when coach at Mansfield Marksmen. Soon after, Paul returned to Station Road a rejuvenated player and continued to improve. He continued to put in some great performances for the Lions and served the club well in the 1987–88 season when the Lions were in rugby league's top flight. Paul played at full-back against the touring Papua New Guinea side in 1987 at Station Road when the Lions won 13–6. He was joined eventually at Swinton by Jim Crellin when he became Swinton's coach in the 1989–90 season. After he left Swinton, Paul went to Oldham where he enjoyed even greater success along with Scott Ranson, another former Swinton player who moved to Watersheddings. At the start of the era of summer rugby in 1996 and 1997, Paul played 33 Super League matches including 10 as substitute for Oldham and in the process scored one try and 19 goals and thereby fulfilling the potential spotted by Jim Crellin a decade earlier.

Mark Welsby was a creative full-back who did a sterling job for the Lions when the club was based at Gigg Lane. Mark signed for Swinton from Wigan on 5 June 1992 and as a result never played for the Lions at Station Road since the move to Bury was announced the previous month. In the first season at Bury, Mark played 27 times scoring 7 tries and one goal. He continued to play for the Lions throughout the 1990s putting in some great displays from full-back and only finishing playing due to a serious hernia injury in 2000. Mark had the potential to play at a higher level and stayed with the Lions for eight years including the 1999 season when he was possibly at his most consistent with a return of 15 tries from 30 appearances. Mark's brother Gary Welsby also played at the club in the 1990s. There have been many comparisons between Mark and Wayne and certainly since the fateful move from Station Road it seems at times that Swinton have only ever had two players in the full-back position such is the apparent seamless transition between the two playing careers. Obviously, this is not true but it is received wisdom in Swinton and Pendlebury that whatever else has happened to the Lions since May 1992 the full-back position has not been the problem. Indeed quite separately, Wayne and Mark have often provided glimpses of genuine talent worthy of any Swinton era.

Of course, there are other players not included in this list who have played well for Swinton at full-back often during difficult times or in an emergency due to injury or dismissal during a game. This selection has been made on the basis of the players' contribution to the club or by virtue of a representative honour. By and large, the previous 22 named full-backs plus Wayne English have all played for Swinton with great distinction in the exposed number one position since the humble beginnings of the club. No doubt there will be much debate about the best Swinton full-back of all time even though historical comparisons are notoriously difficult.

Over the decades there have been many great Swinton full-backs since the pioneering days of the club in the 1860s. Of course, Wayne English plays as a lone full-back unlike in the 1870s when Tom Farr played the position with a partner like half-backs in the modern game. A full-back 100 years ago featured mainly in a defensive role where catching and punting the ball was essential. That is why Arthur Paul was able to convert to a goalkeeper in association football. Alf Chorley did not necessarily have to wear the number one on his back as compulsory numbering of shirts was not introduced in rugby league until 1911. Incidentally, the number one has always been on the shirt of the rugby league full-back similar to the number one for a goalkeeper. (This was also the same in rugby union until the numbering system was inverted in the 1950s so the full-back became number 15.) When Kenny Gowers started his career in 1954 the game had unlimited tackles so a team could sustain pressure in attack for a longer period of time. In today's game the sixth tackle rule means that a team must start attacking as soon as possession is regained. So when Wayne fields a kick on the last tackle he must go on the offensive immediately or else Swinton will lose the initiative. More recently, when Mark Welsby made his Swinton debut, rugby league was still a winter sport played for long periods of the season on heavy pitches. Wayne now plays on surfaces that are much firmer under foot and in hotter temperatures. In spite of the all the differences, from Tom Farr to Wayne English, there has been a continuous line of full-back in the number one shirt of Swinton.

6. Tributes to Wayne English

The following is a selection of tributes about Wayne English from a variety of rugby league books, journals, magazines, newspapers, radio programmes and websites. Also, the section includes a fans' zone at the end as the Swinton supporters show their appreciation of Wayne English.

"Special mention must go to young Wayne English who took the man-of-the-match award [against Waterhead]. Wayne had a shocking injury last season and it's great to see him over that and ready, I'm sure, to make a big impact in the first team."
Mike Gregory, programme notes versus Rochdale Hornets 6 February, 2000

"The recent debut for the Lions by Wayne English gave Swinton players [names] from all the home countries joining Jimmy Irish, Bobby Scott and Harry Welsh."
John Edwards, programme notes versus Keighley Cougars 26 March, 2000

"I went back to Swinton with Featherstone last season and we won a very close game. Swinton are a very under-rated side. They have a lot of good, young lads like Paul Smith and Wayne English who I rate very highly."
Peter Roe speaking in 2000 when coach of Featherstone Rovers

"We also lost Wayne English in the Hunslet game but we are glad to say he has not broken his ankle as was first feared. However, he is in plaster as a precaution and will need to rest a few weeks."
Mike Gregory, programme notes versus Dewsbury Rams 4 March, 2001

"The ex-Widnes players Shea, Fitzy, and Hughes all played well, with Adam [Hughes] picking-up an ankle injury, but he was replaced by Wayne English, who is already a good full-back."
Tony Humphries, programme notes 17 February, 2002

"Game-star: Wayne English. The Lions full-back seemed to be everywhere, in attack he made some dangerous runs and in defence he was there when he had to be." Swinton Lions versus Chorley Lynx, 18 April 2003
Ian Rigg, *Rugby Leaguer & League Express* 19 April 2003

"Game-star: Wayne English. For his superb individual try, sharp running breaks and hard yards achieved." Sheffield Eagles versus Swinton Lions, 9 May 2003
Stuart Charmak, *Rugby Leaguer & League Express* 12 May 2003

"Man-of the-match: Wayne English. Powerful Lions centre Jason Roach scored a great hat-trick and supported man-of-the-match Wayne English wherever he went in search of another try."   Swinton Lions versus York City Knights, 17 August 2003
Ian Rigg, *Rugby Leaguer & League Express* 18 August 2003

"Rugby League World NL2 All-star Team 2004, full-back: Wayne English"
***Gillette Rugby League Yearbook 2004-05* (2004) p. 130**

"The Lions, once again, had a real stand-out player in full-back Wayne English who has been consistently one of the best in the game over recent seasons."
Harry Edgar, *Rugby League Journal Annual* (2005) p. 63

"Full-back Wayne English, winger Marlon Billy and centres Lee Patterson and Chris Maye have almost 100 tries between them this season alone, but it's the two players at the hub of their creation who have been the real stars, Lee Marsh and Phil Joseph."
Richard de la Riviere, *Thirteen: inside Rugby League*, Issue 3 October 2005

"*Rugby League World* NL2 All-star Team 2005, full-back: Wayne English"
***Gillette Rugby League Yearbook 2005-06* (2005) p. 136**

"Hooker or loose forward Phil Joseph won the Young Player of the Year award, and was joined in the NL2 Dream Team by rock-solid full-back Wayne English, powerful wing Marlon Billy and free-scoring stand-off Lee Marsh who broke the club's points-in-a-season record."
***Gillette Rugby League Yearbook 2005-06* (2005) p. 124**

"The money I got brought in the likes of Ian Pickavance, Jon Neill and Phil Veivers – older, wiser, more mature players. These were to complement a relatively young team, with players like Wayne English, Shaun Furey and Mick Nanyn. They were all good, young talent but very raw and I thought the best way forward was to get senior players in who could do the job."
Mike Gregory, *Biting back: the Mike Gregory story* (2006) p. 130

"Wayne English: Number 47 in the top 50 players outside Super League."
***Rugby League World* 2006**

"Stand-off Lee Marsh made a bit of history [in 2005] by beating Albert Blan's Swinton points in a season record, and full-back Wayne English excelled as ever."
Harry Edgar, *Rugby League Journal Annual* (2006) page 61

"The club can announce that 2008 is to be Wayne English's testimonial year. After 10 years, Wayne has earned everyone's respect thanks to his superb efforts during his dedicated tenure with the club. We are sure that all supporters will want to use this period to show their appreciation."
Official Swinton Lions Website 8 December 2007

"As long as I've been involved with the club Wayne has ended the season by walking away with some prize or other. That speaks volumes about the type of player Wayne has been for Swinton. He's part of the fixtures and fittings here."
Paul Kidd, Swinton Lions coach quoted in *League Weekly* December 2007

"Long-serving full-back Wayne English was as good as ever for the Lions with Lee Marsh another star."
Harry Edgar, *Rugby League Journal Annual* (2007) p. 11

"Quicksilver hooker Phil Wood was the Lions stand-out figure throughout, and deservedly cleaned-up at the end of season presentation night. His former Widnes team-mate Bruce Johnson was another player to impress in the front row. Winger Andy Saywell, full-back Wayne English and half-back Craig Ashall and the vastly experienced Martin Moana were also mainstays and the Swinton side."
***Gillette Rugby League Yearbook 2007-08* (2007) page 99**

"You can sense with Wayne English that he is a real professional; someone who is very proud to play for Swinton; very proud of his own performance and you can see that desire and that inner-determination."
Mike Latham, Rugby League presenter, BBC Radio Lancashire 6 February, 2008

"Most players need to prepare fully and they need to eat exactly the same thing the night before a game; they need to eat exactly the same thing for breakfast and they need to arrive at exactly the same time at the ground. But Wayne is one of the few players I've come across at this level who can prepare anyway and still perform at a very, very high level."
Paul Kidd, Swinton Lions coach on BBC Radio Lancashire 6 February, 2008

"Wayne has always been reliable and steadfast for the Lions and he has been coached by Les Holliday, Tony Barrow, Mike Gregory, Peter Roe, Tony Humphries and Paul Kidd. And still Wayne has remained loyal playing the vast majority of his games in the exposed full-back position with great aplomb. This

achievement was recognised in 2006 when Wayne was named in the top 50 players in Britain outside of Super League by the journal Rugby League World."
Ian Jackson, Swinton Lions versus Rochdale Hornets programme, 10 February 2008

"English is a cult hero among Swinton supporters for his unstinting efforts at a club that has often been at the lower end of the Rugby League ladder during his own career. Brave, committed and with no lack of pace or skill, he has long been a scourge of opposition defences in Co-operative National League Two."
Gareth Walker, *Rugby Leaguer and League Express*, Rochdale Hornets v. Swinton Lions programme, 24 February 2008

"To date, he has always decided to remain loyal to the Lions. There is little doubt that Wayne English is Swinton's number one and to mark this feat he has been awarded a testimonial."
Ian Jackson, *Rugby League Review*: Number 2 (2008) p. 39

"Former Widnes duo Bruce Johnson and Phil Wood never let the Lions down during their time on the field, and the likes of Wayne English, Martin Moana and Marlon Billy, who finished with a hugely creditable 18 Tries, deserve credit. But Swinton would set out in 2009 hoping for much more, with Paul Kidd publicly declaring their intensions to mount a serious promotion push"
***Gillette Rugby League Yearbook 2008-09* (2008) page 89**

Wayne English Pen Pictures

The following is a selection of written portraits of Wayne English from various rugby league match-day programmes since 1998.

2008: The current longest serving player and fans favourite. Signed from the Swinton Academy in 1998 after playing his amateur rugby with Kirkholt. Was voted the NL2 all-star team full-back in 2004 and 2005. Has earned a well-deserved testimonial which will take place during the middle of this year.

2007: Full-back. The club's longest serving player and the fans' favourite. Signed from Swinton Academy in 1998 after playing his amateur rugby with Kirkholt. Was voted the NL2 all-stars team full-back for 2004 and 2005.

2006: The club's longest-serving player who arrived through the club's successful Academy under John Prince. A product of the Kirkholt amateur club in Rochdale.

2005: Highly-rated, excels on both attack and defence. Came through the Academy under John Prince and is now the club's longest serving player. [He was] player-of-the-year for the past two seasons.

2004: A promising young player who has scored 14 tries in 23 games this season to rival Chris Maye (15) as the club's top scorer.

2003: Wayne English, full-back, former Rochdale player, although not big, [he is] a promising player. *[Note: the myth that Wayne played for Rochdale Hornets is long-lasting although he did play for the Rochdale town-team as a school-boy.]*

2002: A talented young full-back who progressed to establish himself in the senior side in the previous campaign.

2001: 20-year old full-back, who is a product of the Lions Academy side. Progressed to the senior side last season. A lively attacker and a player still improving.

2000: Wayne English, young full-back who unfortunately suffered a bad injury in 1999. Looking for first-team football in 2000.

Grand Final: Profile. Wayne English is a real stalwart of the Lions. The 26-yearold has been a virtual ever-present in the Swinton number-one shirt in resent times, earning a deserved reputation as one of the most consistent

players in the competition. Dangerous with the ball, an exceptional kick-returner and a solid defender he provides the Lions' rock at the back.
Grand Final Series 2006 8 October, 2006

Chorley: Wayne English (full-back) a promising young player who signed from Rochdale Hornets. *[Note: this is a common misconception that a Rochdale-born player must have signed first for his home-town club. In Wayne's case this assertion is untrue, of course.]*
Chorley Lynx 27 August 2004

Dewsbury: The Lions have one of the best full-backs in the division in Wayne English and he was named in last season's NL2 Dream Team along with team-mates Marlon Billy, Lee Marsh and Phil Joseph. Billy, we know has bags of pace and is a consistent threat out wide especially when Martin Moana is out there on the park.
Dewsbury Rams 20 August 2006

Gateshead: Wayne English, full-back, son of the shop-floor temptress Mollie Sugden and janitor, Arthur English. Wayne gets his style flair and nifty footwork from his Mum and his solid no-nonsense attitude from his Dad who is no pussy himself! *[Note: this is a genuine entry for the Swinton players meant as humorous and light-hearted with no offence intended by the Gateshead programme editor.]*
Gateshead Thunder 14 July 2002

Oldham: Wayne English. An attacking full-back, and the club's longest serving player, 26-year-old English has rattled-up 56 tries in 87 games for the Lions in the past three year, a phenomenal record. A Rochdale boy, he joined Swinton Academy from Kirkholt amateurs when he was 17, and he has never looked back. He was NL2 All-star's full-back in 2004 and 2005 and has remained steadfastly loyal to the Lions despite huge interest from other clubs.
Oldham Rougyeds 18 February 2007

Sheffield: One to watch: Wayne English, the full-back has bags of experience, is totally reliable as the last line of defence, but can also join the attack to telling effect.
Sheffield Eagles 4 July 2004

Swinton: In profile. The arrival of Wayne English into the world of professional rugby league was first recorded in the last ever Rothman's *Rugby League Yearbook*. The nineteenth and final edition in 1999 noted that Wayne signed as an 18 year old for Swinton Lions RLFC on 22 July 1998 from the Kirkholt WMC, an amateur club from the Rochdale area.
Swinton Lions 22 July 2008

Widnes: Top Gun. Wayne English is a Lions stalwart and consistently one of the best full-backs in the lower divisions. He is Swinton's longest serving player and one of the most popular amongst the Lions faithful. A graduate of the Swinton Academy, English is ultra-loyal to the cause and has turned down opportunities to move elsewhere. He was a star for the Lions last year and scored 25 tries from 27 appearances. As reliable as they come at the back and a potent attacking threat, it was little wonder he gained selection in the National League Two All Star team for the second season running. There's little doubt that English is a player worthy of testing himself at a higher level, but Swinton will be delighted that his commitment is firmly to the Lions' cause.
Widnes Vikings 12 February 2006

Whitehaven: A talented young full-back who was Swinton's man-of-the-match as the Lions inflicted a surprise defeat on Whitehaven in the opening game of last season. Progressed to establish himself in the senior side in the previous campaign.
Whitehaven 2 June 2002

Workington: Key Battle: Kamhal Ganley versus Wayne English. The battle of the full-backs looks like a very good contest to watch out for tonight. Kamhal has begun his Workington Town career with some very good performances and has scored seven tries from eight games so far. On the other hand, Wayne English is also an exceptional player with speed and skill and I am surprised he has not moved on to bigger and better things because he has the talent to play at a higher level.
Workington Town 10 May 2006

York: Our visitors' today: His [Paul Kidd's] outstanding full-back, Wayne English has spent much of the season out of action with a broken jaw, returning two weeks ago to a berth on the wing. My admiration for English's mercurial ability is pretty well known and it will be interesting to see how he goes today and in what position.
York City Knights 27 July 2008

Wayne English: Swinton highlights

RL Season	Swinton Coach	Home Ground	Season Highlight
1998	Les Holliday	Gigg Lane	Signing professionally for the Lions
1999	Les Holliday Mike Gregory	Gigg Lane	Recovering fully from knee surgery
2000	Mike Gregory	Gigg Lane	First Team Debut versus Waterhead
2001	Mike Gregory	Gigg Lane	Making Progress in the first-team squad
2002	Tony Humphries Phil Veivers	Gigg Lane Moor Lane	Reaching the Elimination Play-off
2003	Peter Roe	Moor Lane	Cup Quarter-Final & NL2 Select v. NZ 'A'
2004	Paul Kidd	Park Lane	Selection for the All-Star Team 2004
2005	Paul Kidd	Park Lane	Selection for the All-Star Team 2005
2006	Paul Kidd	Park Lane	Play-off Series and The Grand Final
2007	Paul Kidd	Park Lane	Reaching the Elimination Play-off
2008	Paul Kidd	Park Lane	Award of the Ten-year Testimonial

No introductions needed: Wayne meets former Lion Jason Roach (Blackpool) at Park Lane 19 February 2006

Extracts from Wayne's scrap-book

Many thanks are due to Betty Taylor (Grandma English) for keeping a scrap-book of her grandson's Rugby League career from the early days at Kirkholt.

2000

"Two minutes later a good run down the left wing by Wayne English created the opportunity for Paul Smith to touch down with Watson again adding the goal points."
Bury Times, Mike Cain, April 2000.

"The try of the game came on the 65 minute. An Oldham kick over the Lions line was taken by English, who raced 50 metres down the left wing before being halted. Quick passing saw Roach crossing in the right-hand corner."
Bury Times, Mike Cain, April 2000.

"After Wayne English hauled down [Sheffield] Eagles forward David Larder in mid-field, the Lions worked the ball up to the other end and a Watson bomb-kick was collected by Mick Nanyn who put Richard Henare through a gap to touch-down behind the posts."
Bury Times, Mike Cain, April 2000.

"A towering 40-20 kick from Watson enabled the Lions to set up the position for a wonderful try by Wayne English."
Bury Times, Mike Cain, April 2000.

"[Featherstone] Rovers coach [Peter] Roe 'I went back to Swinton with Featherstone last season and we won a very close game. It will be a tough fixture for us on Monday. Swinton are a very under-rated side. They have a lot of good, young lads like Paul Smith and Wayne English who I rate very highly.'"
Bury Times, Steve Bott, April 2000.

"Wayne English saved the Lions once more with a great run out of defence."
Bury Times, Mike Cain, June 2000.

"English capped a fine personal performance by scooping the loose Watson pass off the floor and going behind the [York] posts."
Bury Times, Mike Cain, June 2000.

2001

"Swinton full-back has his hands full trying to stop opposite number Brett Mullins during the [Challenge Cup] game against Leeds."
Bury Times, Steve Bott, February 2001.

"Lions substitute Wayne English almost brought some light relief when he looked to be heading to score two minutes into the second half but his juggling act with the ball behind his back simple had the crowd either moaning or sniggering as he finally dropped the ball going over the Batley line."
Bury Times, Steve Bott, April 2001.

2002
"Frantically trying to get back in the game, Wayne English's defensive mistake let in [Batley's] Paul Glendhill to score a try converted by Lawford to make it 32-16."
Salford Advertiser, Marc Iles, Thursday 20 June 2002.

"So the die is cast. The Rugby League has inspected Moor Lane and pronounced it fit for human consumption. Swinton will return to home turf or something adjacent to it next month."
Match-day Programme, Dave Hadfield, 5 July 2002.

"Once again the pendulum swung the way of Swinton when Wayne English showed superb pace to score in the corner [against Barrow]."
Salford Advertiser, Marc Iles, Thursday 11 July 2002.

"Moor Lane is not exactly the McAlpine Stadium, and it's not quite the in the centre of town, but the club has returned as close to its roots as it's possible to get, and we now have a place we can call home."
Match-day Programme, Simon Kelner, 4 August 2002.

2003
"The first score of the match arrived nine minutes in and it came to the Lions when Craig Wingfield sent Wayne English through a huge gap in the [Featherstone] Rovers defence and Phil Hassan was in support to take the pass and race 30 metres to score."
Rugby Leaguer & League Express, Ian Rigg, 3 March 2003.

"The Lions second try came when Peter Cannon and [Chris] Hough combined well to send full-back Wayne English racing over towards the left-hand corner."
Rugby Leaguer & League Express, Ian Rigg, 3 March 2003.

"Swinton, perhaps with half an eye on next week's visit to Wigan were a huge disappointment on a ground [Whitehaven's Recreation Ground] where they have a particularly impressive record in recent years. Unattractively attired in a slate grey kit to match the day, they looked like hapless refugees from some Sunday Morning Soccer League. Unfortunately for them and their hardy bunch of followers they also played like hapless refugees from some Sunday morning

soccer league. Most of the game took place in their half of the field and their play was littered with handling errors."
Rugby Leaguer & League Express, Stephen Bowes, 10 March 2003.

"There was no let up from Wigan after the re-start when English knocked-on in the first minute of the [second] half, and from the resulting scrum Bibey barged his way over after some pressure on the Lions line."
Rugby Leaguer & League Express, Ian Rigg, 17 March 2003.

"When the final hooter sounded, the Lions went to their supporters to offer their thanks and took a deserved ovation from both sets of fans as they left the [JJB] pitch."
Rugby Leaguer & League Express, Ian Rigg, 17 March 2003.

"It's a tribute to the spirit instilled by Peter Roe that despite the inevitable parade of tries from star-studded Wigan, the Lions never stopped tackling and working – typified by the wholehearted way Wayne English hurled himself at David Hodgson in a brave attempt to deny the Warriors their 13th and final try."
Salford Advertiser, Claire Mooney, Thursday 20 March 2003.

"His [Martin Hall] counterpart Roe felt a couple of crucial decisions went against his side in the second period, as impressive full-back Wayne English was adjudged to have knocked the ball on over the line and was pulled back for a knock-on that was difficult to spot from the stands."
Rugby Leaguer & League Express, Gareth Walker, 24 March 2003.

"Game-star Wayne English was one, along with the half-backs, whose lively runs gained huge amounts of territory throughout the match. He exposed the [Sheffield] Eagles' poor defence explicitly when he took the ball from a scrum. He ran along the line right to left, evaded pathetic grabs, rounded the winger and hoofed it along the touch-line to score behind the posts."
Rugby Leaguer & League Express, Stuart Charmak, 10 May 2003.

2004
"English went very close in the 50th minute when he beat at least six [Workington] Town players but lost the ball as he went over the line."
Match-day Programme, Ian Rigg, 1 August 2004.

"Rob Whittaker was next over the [Chorley] line when he scored with his first touch of the ball having got a good shot pass from English."
Match day Programme, Ian Rigg, 5 September 2004.

"The Lions levelled the scores [against Workington Town in the play-offs] five minutes later when Ian Sinfield and Kris Smith combined to send Wayne English in for the try and Paul Ashton added the goal points."
Swinton Lions website, Ian Rigg, 20 September 2004.

2005

"Wayne English put the Lions back in the lead four minutes after the break when, from a scrum near the [Hunslet] Hawks line, English took on three defenders to wriggle over in the corner and again Coates' conversion fell just wide of the posts."
Match day Programme, Ian Rigg, 12 June 2005.

"The Lions hit back again six minutes from time when Wayne English jinked through the [Workington] Town defence to go over in the left corner but again Marsh was unable to convert against the wind and Town held on just for victory."
Match day Programme, Ian Rigg, 10 July 2005.

"Tim Gee almost put the [London] Skolars ahead again but Wayne English won the foot race to the line to stop the danger."
Match day Programme, Ian Rigg, 7 August 2005.

2006

"Wayne English and Marlon Billy pulled off try-saving tackles [against Featherstone Rovers] before Paul Alcock and Andy Saywell touched down to give the Lions an 8-2 half-time lead."
Salford Advertiser, Jeff Tyldesley, 28 September 2006.

They [Celtic Crusaders] had the chance to take the lead late on in the first half when Wayne English knocked-on perilously close to his line, but Crusaders failed to take advantage as Hywel Davies did likewise from the second play."
Rugby Leaguer & League Express, Ian Golden 2 October 2006

"The bravery of Swinton's full-back, Wayne English, had prevented the [Sheffield] Eagles from breaking through until then, notably when he knocked the ball from James Ford's clutches as he dived over the line."
The Independent, Mike Latham, 9 October 2006.

2007

"Hooker Phil Wood and full-back Wayne English were as lively as ever and Darren Woods provided a master-class of centre play. He scored two tries and had a length of the field score harshly disallowed for off-side. Swinton's other try scorers in a see-saw affair which was pleasing to the eye where English, Wood,

Martin Moana, Conway, Smith and Walker [against Salford in a pre-season friendly game].
Salford Advertiser, Dave Lawrenson, 8 February 2007.

"Swinton swept into a 10–0 lead [against Oldham] with Liam McGovern's kick setting-up a try for Wayne English and Andy Saywell re-gathering his own kick to score a fine solo effort."
Salford Advertiser, Claire Mooney, 12 July 2007.

"Lions full-back Wayne English fumbled the wet ball to hand Hunslet the first score which saw Mark Moxon going over off Dave Foster's pass."
Salford Advertiser, Claire Mooney, 6 September 2007.

2008
"Wayne English jinked as ever across the defensive link and a nice outside ball allowed Dean Gorton to race through but remarkable [Oldham] cover from Paul O'Connor brought him down."
Salford Advertiser, Jeff Tyldesley, Thursday 24 April 2008.

"The Lions always find it tough at Derwent Park. Their dreadful record there suggests that Swinton are jinxed at the home of Workington Town. So the last thing they needed was to go into Sunday's game missing several players through injury. And the task was made doubly difficult by Wayne English, Neil Rigby and Dean Gorton all picking up injuries during the course of the match."
Salford Advertiser, Jeff Tyldesley, Thursday 1 May 2008.

"Swinton Lions hope to have full-back Wayne English back from a broken jaw for the clash with Doncaster on Wednesday night. Bruce Johnson has a one-match ban, but Marlon Billy can play."
Manchester Evening News Tuesday 8 July 2008.

"It started so positively, [against London Skolars] Rob Line steam-rollered over Mario Du Toit to score from 10 yards out before an excellent cut out pass from Martin Moana created enough space for Wayne English to race in."
Salford Advertiser, Jeff Tyldesley, Thursday 17 July 2008.

"The Lions got off to a dream start [against Hunslet] with man-of-the-match English, Marlon Billy and Martin Moana all touching down in the first 22 minutes of the game. Liam McGovern touched down following good work by Gary Sykes, English and Gary Hulse; Dean Gorton gobbled-up a chance offered to him by English's reverse pass…"
Salford Advertiser, Dave Lawrenson, Thursday 7 August 2008.

Six little known things about Wayne English

1. Wayne never played for Rochdale Hornets before signing professionally for Swinton Lions in July 1998.

2. Wayne's professional Rugby League career was almost over before it began following a serious injury in 1999 when he snapped a cruciate ligament and had to have knee reconstruction surgery. He was out of action for almost a year.

3. Although Wayne is not very superstitious, he always wears his socks inside-out during a game. He has consistently done this throughout his career.

4. Wayne English has been sent-off only once in his professional career during a league match against London Skolars at the New River Stadium in the capital in 2003. He was found guilty by the RFL of running in and striking; he received a two match ban and also fined £75.

5. Wayne's favourite match is the league game at home to York on 17 August 2003 because it was the day after his daughter Alicia was born.

6. Wayne English is wrongly credited in the record books as the scorer of the drop-goal in the game between the National League Two Select and New Zealand 'A' at Keighley in 2005. The scorer was in fact Swinton team-mate Chris Hough. The match reporter must have misread Chris' number 6 for Wayne's number 1.

Wayne English by John Thomason, former development manager

As Swinton's longest serving player, Wayne English started his career with the club 10 years ago, but his roots in rugby league stretch back much further than his first appearance of 201 first team starts for the Lions.

"When I first started I was about nine." recalled Wayne, who hails from Rochdale. "My school didn't have a rugby team, so like many lads my age I played locally for one of the town's clubs."

As a young player, Wayne wore shirts for a number of clubs in the area, before being selected for the Rochdale town team and, in time, representing Lancashire on a number of occasions.

"It was great to make that step-up" continued Wayne. "I was in the county squad amongst lads like Neil Turley and Dwayne West, who both ended up making an impact in the National League and the Super League".

The value of the representative structures in the community game was something appreciated by Wayne. "It proves you're doing well for your team. It is an honour to be asked to play for someone else."

Much of Wayne's early rugby was played with the Kirkholt club in Rochdale. "Before signing for Swinton, my last game for Kirkholt was in a sevens competition" said Wayne who, still a teenager, captained the open-age side in the Mayfield 7s tournament. "We won the tournament, which was a great result; a great send-off for me before I came to Swinton. I'm still very close to a lot of the Kirkholt players. There are some good lads there."

"When I was 16, John Prince asked me to come to the Lions. At first I was a bit taken aback by the size of some of the guys at the club, but I knew that I was going to have to work extra hard to make an impact at this level. I had to prove that I could play."

Growing up in the 1980s and 1990s, Wayne's heroes in the game were inevitably influenced by the great Wigan sides of that time, players like Offiah, Hanley and Robinson, but John Prince also made an impact on Wayne.

"He took me under his wing and taught me how to conduct myself as a professional. He was the stand-out guy, and this stood me in good stead when I eventually made it into the first-team."

Wayne's route via the Rochdale junior game, through Swinton Academy and into first-team was typical of many contemporaries, although what set Wayne apart from the others was his pride in the blue and white shirt and loyalty to the Lions and the supporters. At a time when testimonials outside Super League are few and far between, Wayne began a career that made him a firm favourite with parents and juniors alike.

"My first game for the first-team was against Waterhead in the Challenge Cup. I wanted to show people that I was good enough to play for Swinton and in that game I tried my hardest."

That game, on 1 February 2000, saw the Lions beat the Oldham amateurs by 74 points to a single drop goal, with Wayne scoring one of the sixteen tries that day.

It was under the supervision of the late Mike Gregory that he broke through to the first-team in 2000, and after the Challenge Cup game against Waterhead, Wayne made a further fourteen appearances for the Lions that season, becoming a regular start on the team-sheet and scoring three further tries over the next few months. "Greg was a stand-out guy, and he was a great player." said the full-back. "He was prepared to chuck me in at the deep end and gave me my chance. I don't think he'd have done that if he didn't think I could do the job."

The club has had some great games over the last 10 years, everything from exciting Challenge Cup draws, through to the Co-operative National League Two Grand Final at Warrington, and Wayne has certainly played his part in many of these big days.

The 2003 Challenge Cup season was certainly memorable, as the Lions progressed to the last eight after seeing off Shaw Cross, Chorley Lynx and Featherstone Rovers in previous rounds.

"The Challenge Cup Quarter final game against Wigan was a great day for club and for the fans. It was an experience to be part of that atmosphere." With over 5,000 fans in the JJB Stadium, many wearing blue and white, it was certainly a day for all to enjoy, especially after Rob Russell crossed after just nine minutes to put the Lions 4—0 up, with a further two points converted by Chris Hough. The lead was held for over quarter of an hour, when the full-time fitness of a world-class Wigan led to a 70–12 victory for the Riversiders, a side coached by Stuart Raper, with Wayne's mentor, Mike Gregory as his assistant.

The 2003 season saw Wayne begin to reach his full potential at the Lions, making thirty appearances out of thirty two fixtures. Indeed, from 2003 to 2007 Wayne made 145 appearances for the Lions out of a total of 156 played, only two of which saw him coming off the bench which is a fantastic track record that was only hit in 2008 by an unfortunate injury.

In 2005 Wayne racked up a century of points with the Lions, scoring 25 tries in 27 appearances, putting his overall tally well on the way to 300. Wayne continued assessing more recent times with the 2006 play-offs. It had been a long season for the Lions, in total they would play 35 games, 33 of which would feature Wayne and finishing fifth in the league gave the squad a tough run towards the final. "The run-in against Featherstone and Celtic Crusaders was fantastic, and the golden point victory at Brewery Field was superb. These games gave us a great confidence boost. We knew we had it in us, and the games gave us the ultimate feeling of belonging to a team. All the lads worked for each other in those games."

The big games also gave Wayne the opportunity to play against some of the leading talents in Rugby League. "I've played against guys that have played State of Origin, and despite the bad result against Leeds, it was an experience to play against world class players like Iestyn Harris."

Wayne had similar thoughts on some of his team-mates at Swinton. "I enjoyed playing alongside Peter Cannon, Phil Veivers and Simon Knox. They helped out a lot when they were at the club, all players who were at the close of their careers, but helped out a lot when I was really just starting out in the professional game."

Perhaps surprisingly one of Wayne's favourite grounds was a little closer to home. "I enjoyed Moor Lane, even though the facilities weren't that great. It was a tight ground with a quality pitch, and it generated a good little atmosphere."

"I enjoyed playing in the fixtures at Widnes, too. It was a good crowd in a compact ground with a nice pitch. Gigg Lane was good at the start too. It's been a great few years at Swinton, and my ambition with the club would be to be involved at National League One level and to get promotion." finished Wayne.

"My own ambitions within the game might one day involve coaching. I coached Whitworth under-12s a few years back, and I'd like to be involved in the junior game again. Rugby league has been my life since I was nine years old and I'd like to pass something on."

Now and then interviews

The answers from 2002 are taken from the Swinton Lions v. Barrow Raiders programme 5 July 2002. Six years later on 28 May 2008 at the White Lion in Swinton the same questions were asked with the previous answers concealed from Wayne. The 2008 answers like Wayne's performances are remarkably consistent, but do offer some variation and some interesting insights as well.

Question	2002	2008
Marital Status	Single	Engaged
Occupation	Window maker	Welder
Position	Full-back	Full-back
Hardest player	Tonie Carroll	Tonie Carroll
Superstitions	Wear socks inside out	Wear socks inside out
Likes	Socialising with friends	Socialising with friends
Dislikes	Losing at rugby	Spiders
Greatest influence	Family and former coaches	Parents
Career highlight	Signing pro	The Grand Final 2006
Car	Rover 214 si	Ford Focus
Favourite food	Peppered steak	Peppered steak
Favourite drink	Lucozade Sport	Lager

The fans' zone: memories of Wayne from the terraces

One of the tries that stands out for me is against Hunslet in the 2005 National League Two playoffs. Wayne skipped past two Hunslet players before lifting his fist in the air then putting the ball down for the winning try.
Paul Thomason, Swinton

The way Wayne returned from injury after breaking his jaw in 2008 was a real credit to him. He was out for over two months after he sustained the injury by accident when making a brave tackle at Workington in May. By the end of the season he was back to his best and even scored three tries in the final five matches.
Garry Jackson, Worsley

The first time I spoke to Wayne was in 2004 at the South Leeds Stadium after a match against Hunslet. He was happy to sign my ticket and stay and chat to the fans.
Paul Thomason, Swinton

I am a ball-boy at Swinton and it's great to watch Wayne from such close range. You can hear him crunch into tackles. Also, Wayne sometimes whistles through his teeth to his team-mates in order to get their attention.
Thomas Jackson, Macclesfield

You'll never beat Wayne English.
Chant of the Swinton Beer People

It is so rare for Wayne to make a major mistake that when he does you remember it. In 2006 against Dewsbury at Park Lane he dropped the ball in his own in-goal area in the dying seconds of the match after the Lions had just taken the lead. Dewsbury scored and won the game, but no-one blamed Wayne for the defeat because of his all round contribution to the team.
Phil Poole, Stoke-on-Trent

I remember well one incident in a National League Cup match against Batley at home in 2005. Swinton were attacking up the slope towards the clubhouse end when Batley regained possession and their winger made a dash down the popular side. He had a head start on Wayne who not only caught-up with him before the halfway line, but also dump-tackled him into touch for good measure. Someone in the crowd shouted to the Batley player: "You'll never beat Wayne English!" and he gave them a really dirty look, but he didn't disagree.
Stuart MacDonald, Swinton

I am 10 years old and I've been to over 150 Swinton games. Wayne is my favourite player and he has played since I can remember.
George Jackson, Macclesfield

As a Swinton supporter, you are always reassured to see Wayne's name on the team-sheet.
Kath Tyldesley, Manchester

Wayne, Wayne, Wayne, Wayne, Wayne...
Chant of the Swinton Beer People

I once caught Wayne by surprise at Sharm-el-Sheikh airport. He probably did not expect to be recognised in Egypt even though he was wearing his testimonial shirt. Actually, I recognised him before I saw the shirt. I asked him how the testimonial was going and told him that I hoped for a better 2009 season.
Ray Cresswell, Bury

When my eldest son Tom was about nine years old he was the Swinton mascot on his birthday at the Moor Lane ground. He was waiting outside the changing rooms with club captain Simon Knox ready to lead the team out onto the pitch. Simon asked Tom who his favourite player was and of course he replied "Wayne English." Simon laughed and replied "I'll soon put you right!"
Ian Jackson, Macclesfield

Wayne is so loyal to Swinton that he can't keep away from the club. On one occasion a few years back he was rested for an away fixture at Oldham following a long uninterrupted spell in the first team. Most players would have taken the opportunity to have a complete break but Wayne turned up to watch the game and sat with his family next to the Swinton supporters.
Paul Davidson, Worsley

I saw Wayne in the players' lounge after the Dewsbury game when his mistake cost us the game late on. His head was sunk low into his chest. I told his partner Nina to tell him to cheer up as it was just one of those things that happen in rugby league, especially when you are a whole-hearted player like Wayne.
Mike Cain, Pendlebury

I was a regular visitor to Station Road to watch the old 'A' team but due to working away, then moving away I only got to one Academy match in the depressing Gigg Lane days. It was an evening match against Keighley and played at Radcliffe Borough FC. I took along my son and his best mate and saw an emphatic Swinton victory. Two things I still remember about that game, firstly how good a game the ref had and secondly a solo "Danny Wilson" style

try from the young full-back. I'm sure I remember rightly that Wayne signed the next night and has gone on to be the best servant the club has had in the post-Station Road days. His contributions since then have been the reason why a lot of us keep going. He's been an inspiration through our not so good times and no-one deserves our support more.
Martin McDonough, Wardley

Some of the lads were having a laugh with Wayne outside the team-bus at Doncaster and when he went to get on board the driver didn't open the door for him at first. He must have thought Wayne was one of the supporters.
Rick Smith, Mosley Common

In my experience only one rugby league coach has really managed to play effectively against the unpredictability of Wayne English; and that's Peter Roe. He brought a Barrow side in 2007 to Park Lane with a game plan that marginalized Wayne.
Mike Cain, Pendlebury

You always get 100% from Wayne English.
Trevor Harvey, Swinton

Peter Roe is a really formidable coach and someone who stands no messing about when things get serious. During one important team talk in 2003, kit-man Eric Skeech accidentally stood on a yard brush and the handle hit him on the head. Even though the Moor Lane changing rooms are tiny, Wayne was the only person who saw what had happened. Luckily for him, he just about managed not to laugh out loud and so narrowly escaped the wrath of Roey.
Mike Cain, Pendlebury

The best tackle I ever saw Wayne make was during the Grand Final in 2006 when he seemed to punch the ball from the grasp of a Sheffield Eagles player as he was about to score a try.
James Jackson, Worsley

Personification of Swinton by Jeff Tyldesley, life-long supporter

Straight to the point, Wayne English reflects what Swinton Lions RLFC is in these modern times of Rugby League; namely small but certainly capable of punching above our weight. I actually believe what has held Wayne back from playing for more heavyweight outfits in higher leagues has been his height and size, ironically what holds back the club itself from playing in the upper echelons of the game.

Wayne has been one of the most exciting rugby league players to grace the National Leagues over the past couple of decades. His ability to explode from a standing start through a packed defence with just the drop of a shoulder here and a shimmy there has been truly thrilling to watch. This, coupled with superb execution of brave tackling, and being able to haul down forwards seemingly two or three times his bulk have rendered him one of the most reliable performers around.

In his decade with Swinton, Wayne has been linked with numerous clubs but somehow almost miraculously he has stayed with the Lions. A National League Two Grand Final in 2006 (and *en route* the world's first extra time golden-point victory in Bridgend) were his biggest reward for all his toil.

Undoubtedly, he could have accrued more money, fame and glory playing for Widnes, Salford or Oldham, even below Super League, but yet he has stuck with us, even at our lowest ebb, finishing 10th in the 2008 National League Two and being asked to play in an alien position on the wing, where he still far from disgraced himself. To think 10 years ago, it only took 80 minutes for him to announce himself on the rugby league scene, claiming a try on his debut, a cup tie in 2000 against Waterhead, where he won man-of-the-match.

Finally, the Lions had discovered a long term successor at the vital position of full-back to Mark Welsby, arguably the most talented individual to have worn the blue and white since the club decamped from Station Road. Similar to Welsby, a quirk of fate, like the back injury in Welsby's case, his lack of height has apparently prevented him from playing in a higher league so he has served Swinton for a long time with great distinction.

A sign of a good player is if opposition fans rate him or ask whether he is in the team or not. Wayne is frequently mentioned as you wander through the various grounds Swinton have inhabited. "English isn't playing, we stand a chance today…" Again, the "If only he was a few inches taller…" criticism remains, too!

Another sign of a good player is whether the fans chant his name and it goes beyond the customary "There's only one Mr X". Wayne saw numerous incantations based around him varying from: "You'll never beat Wayne English" to the sacrilegious "Wayne English, my Lord, Wayne English!"

Of all the players that have departed Swinton for the lure of the Super League and full-time contracts in recent times, Jordan James, Mick Nanyn, Karl Fitzpatrick, Andy Coley, the list could go on, and not one other player has seen a banner created begging him to stay! In Wayne's case, this was not just at one end of the season game but two!

He has cleared the board at Swinton's end of season awards more than he can probably remember; it's heartening for the supporters to see a player almost embarrassed at the accolades. Speeches that start thanking everyone but himself in the team and end in just a sheepish "Thanks!" before refusing to say anymore!

In fact, the most uncomfortable I've seen him performing a task in the name of Swinton Lions was at his own testimonial's Question and Answer session in 2008 when a drunken supporter's question (and in some cases statements about his brother being in the Red Arrows and being a ball-boy at Station Road!) left him looking baffled beyond words!

If, like many believe, these are the final days of Swinton Lions RLFC's proud history and the end of provincial northern town teams in general in an era of franchising and "big cities", I certainly hope the contribution of the likes of Wayne are as highly regarded in the future as the players from the championship and five cup winning sides of the eras before him.

For Swinton as a club, the odds are now stacked against us but it shouldn't stop in revering a great player who's played in several mixed quality teams. As a fan, you couldn't ask for any more, Wayne's played above and beyond his weight for many years with undoubted commitment, through the bad times and the good, in his ideal position and alien ones like being the left-winger. That's all you can ask.

Like Swinton, Wayne is underestimated, if his true value was realised, he wouldn't still be here! For this outcome we are very thankful. In short, as a supporter, I'd like to say thanks and all the best in everything you do after finishing playing the game.

The final contribution goes deservedly to John Spellman who has not missed a Swinton game since 14 October 1979 and therefore has seen every moment of Wayne's career with the Lions.

Wayne English: A poem by Spelly

I know he lives in Rochdale,
But he's Swinton to the core,
He never takes a backward step,
And he makes the Lions roar!

For ten years, he's been with us,
And now it's testimonial time,
So I knocked these words together,
And put them all to rhyme!

A real attacking full-back,
And as a tackler, there's none meaner,
His lady's is one special girl
That's the very pretty, Nina!

A decade as a Lion,
Always doing a first-class job,
Let's hope this year long effort,
Makes him (more than) a few bob!

The Junior Lions love him,
He's their superstar,
Especially when he touches down,
Right underneath the bar!

But to **all** Lions fans he's a winner,
To oppositions, he's a pain,
So I wrote this poem just to say,
Thanks a million Wayne!

Spelly!

"...and then on the eighth day, God created Rugby League."

Who says Wayne can't pass? In action against Hunslet in 2007

Considering his options against Keighley in 2007

References

Edgar, Harry (2005), *Rugby League Journal Annual 2005*
Edgar, Harry (2006), *Rugby League Journal Annual 2006*
Edgar, Harry (2007). *Rugby League Journal Annual 2007*
Edgar, Harry (2008), *Rugby League Journal Annual 2008*
Farrar, Dave and Lush, Peter (2008), *Rugby League Review: Number Two*
Giggs, Ryan (2006), *Giggs: the autobiography*
Gillette Rugby League Yearbook 2005-2006
Gillette Rugby League Yearbook 2006-2007
Gillette Rugby League Yearbook 2007-2008
Gillette Rugby League Yearbook 2008-2009
Gregory, Mike *et al.* (2006), *Biting Back: The Mike Gregory Story*
Hadfield, Dave (2004), *Up and over: a trek through Rugby League land*
Inglis, Simon (2004), *Played in Manchester: the architectural heritage of a city at play*
Kuzio, David (2006), *We'll support you evermore: Rugby League fans' memories*
Latham, Mike (2005), *A ground-hopper's guide to British Rugby League*
League Express Rugby League Yearbook 1999-2000
League Express Rugby League Yearbook 2000-2001
League Express Rugby League Yearbook 2001-2002
League Express Rugby League Yearbook 2002-2003
League Express Rugby League Yearbook 2003-2004
League Express Rugby League Yearbook 2004-2005
Rothman's Rugby League Yearbook 1999 Edition
Wild, Stephen (1999), *The Lions of Swinton: a complete history*
Wild, Stephen (2002), *Swinton Rugby League Football Club*

Appendices

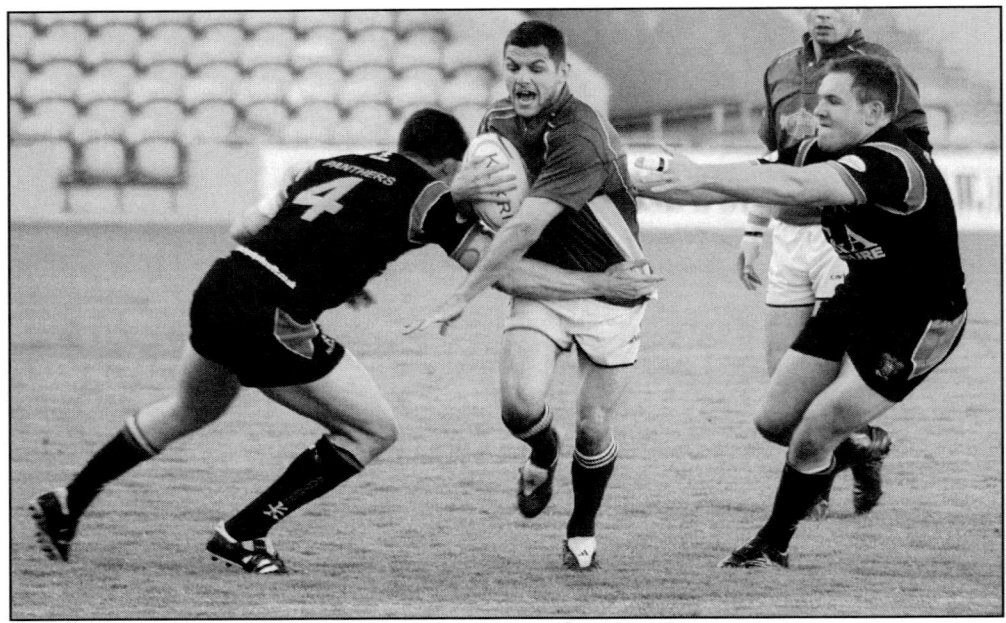

Wayne battles through the Blackpool defence
at Bloomfield Road with Ian Sinfield in support

Appendix A: Wayne English summary from 2000 to 2008

Season	App: Starts + Sub	Tries	Points
2000	12+3	5	20
2001	15+3	4	16
2002	13+4	5	20
2003	30	8	32
2004	27	17	68
2005	27	25	100
2006	33+1	14	56
2007	28+1	8	32
2008	16	6	24
Total	201+12	92	368

Appendix B: Swinton Lions summary from 1999 to 2008

Season (games)	Most Apps	Top Try scorer	Top Goal scorer	Top point scorer
1999 (30)	Ian Watson & Mark Welsby (30)	Mark Welsby (15)	Ian Watson (58)	Ian Watson (143)
2000 (30)	Paul Smith (29)	Phil Coussons (18)	Ian Watson (84)	Ian Watson (190)
2001 (30)	Rob Barraclough & Mick Nanyn (29)	Paul Smith (16)	Mick Nanyn (72)	Mick Nanyn (204)
2002 (35)	Lee Hansen (32+2)	Mick Nanyn (15)	Mick Nanyn (62)	Mick Nanyn (184)
2003 (32)	Wayne English (30)	Jason Roach (17)	Chris Hough (86)	Chris Hough (208)
2004 (28)	Wayne English (27)	Chris Maye (21)	Paul Ashton & Warren Ayres (37)	Warren Ayres (96)
2005 (30)	Lee Patterson (30)	Marlon Billy (26)	Lee Marsh (114)	Lee Marsh (310)
2006 (35)	Wayne English (33+1)	Andy Saywell (26)	Lee Marsh (41)	Lee Marsh (112)
2007 (32)	Wayne English (28+1)	Andy Saywell (21)	Lee Marsh (61)	Lee Marsh (150)
2008 (30)	Rob Line* (26+1)	Marlon Billy (18)	Richie Hawkyard (47)	Richie Hawkyard (106)

*Martin Moana made 18 starts plus 12 as substitute.

Appendix C: Swinton Lions match-by-match from 1999 to 2008

Season 1999

31-01-99	Moldgreen (Huddersfield) CC3 Gigg Lane W 38-4 G: S. Gartland 5; T: Ashcroft 3, Stazicker, Taylor, McCabe, Watson
7-02-99	Hunslet NFP Gigg Lane L10-21 G: S Gartland T: Ashcroft, Welsby
14-02-99	Huddersfield CC4 McAlpine Stadium L78-4 T: Stazicker
21-02-99	Doncaster NFP Belle Vue L22-18 G: Watson 2, S Gartland; T: P. Barrow, Blease, Evans
7-03-99	Bramley NFP Gigg Lane W23-8 G: S. Garland 1+1dg, Watson 4; T: Cleary, McCabe, Eccles
14-03-99	York NFP Huntington Stadium L16-15 G: S Gartland, Watson 1dg; T: Billy, Evans, S. Gartland
21-03-99	Dewsbury NFP Gigg Lane L19-29 G: Watson 3+1dg T: Cleary, Hill, Henare
28-03-99	Whitehaven NFP Recreation Ground W4-12 G: Watson 2; T: Watson, S Gartland
2-04-99	Rochdale Hornets NFP Gigg Lane W 28-24 G: Watson 4 T: Price-Jones, Rogers, McCabe, Henare, Stevens
5-04-99	Featherstone Rovers NFP Post Office Road L50-20 G: Watson 4 T: Henare, Eccles, Casey
11-04-99	Barrow NFP Gigg Lane L24-31 G: S Gartland 4; T: Price-Jones, Henare, P Barrow, Cushion
18-04-99	Widnes NFP Naughton Park L25-10 G: S Gartland; T: Welsby, Casey
25-04-99	Leigh NFP Gigg Lane L22-34 G: S Gartland 5; T: Welsby, Ashcroft, Taylor
9-05-99	Lancashire Lynx NFP Victory Park W10-56 G: S Gartland 5, Watson 3; T: Casey 2, S Gartland 2, Henare, Ashcroft, Hill, Welsby, P Barrow, Cushion,
16-05-99	Keighley NFP Gigg Lane L14-15 G: S. Gartland 3; T: P. Barrow, Casey
23-05-99	Oldham NFP Gigg Lane W31-24 G: S. Gartland 5, Casey 1dg; T: Rogers 2, Billy 2, Bateman
30-05-99	Workington Town NFP Derwent Park L37-20 G: S Gartland 4; T: Smith, S Gartland, Casey
13-06-99	Hull KR NFP New Craven Park L30-10 G: S Gartland; T: Welsby, Casey
20-06-99	Hunslet NFP South Leeds Stadium L22-8 T: P. Gartland, Welsby
27-06-99	Doncaster NFP Gigg Lane W48-2 G: S Gartland 6 T: Welsby 3, Hunter, Billy, Eyres, Bateman, Ashcroft, Evans
4-07-99	Bramley NFP Headingley L20-14 G: S Gartland 3 T: Billy, P. Barrow
7-07-99	Batley NFP Gigg Lane W23-14 G: Watson 2+2dg, Casey 1dg; T: Hill, Eyres, Welsby, Henare
11-07-99	York NFP Gigg Lane W23-12 G: Watson 5, Casey 1dg; T: Henare, Casey, P. Gartland
18-07-99	Dewsbury NFP New Crown Flatt L27-26 G: Watson 5 T: Welsby, P. Barrow, Cleary, Hill
25-07-99	Whitehaven NFP Gigg Lane W51-28 G: Watson 7+1dg T: Henare 3, Welsby 2, Watson, S Gartland, Smith, Hill
1-08-99	Rochdale Hornets NFP Spotland Stadium L 32-29 G: Watson 4 +1dg; T: Eccles, Welsby, Smith, Eyres, Cleary
8-08-99	Featherstone Rovers NFP Gigg Lane L22-24 G: Watson 5; T: Bateman, Hill, Evans
15-08-99	Barrow NFP Craven Park W14-33 G: Watson 4+1dg; T: Watson 2, Nanyn 2, Evans, Cleary
22-08-99	Widnes NFP Gigg Lane L16-44 G: Watson 2; T: Eccles, Watson, Henare
29-08-99	Leigh NFP Hilton Park L22-20 G: Watson 2; T: Johnson 2, Welsby, Bateman

Season 2000

26-12-99	Workington Town NFP Derwent Park W 21-10 G: Watson 2, Casey 1dg; T: Billy, Loughlin, Bateman, Roach
2-1-00	Oldham NFP Gigg Lane L18-23 G: Watson 3; T: Smith, Coussons, Bateman
9-1-00	Leigh NFP Hilton Park W20-22 G: Watson 3; T: Smith 2, Coussons, Coley
16-1-00	Lancashire Lynx NFP Gigg Lane W54-6 G: Watson 7; T: Loughlin 3, Coley 2, Pickavance 2, Craig, Watson, Billy
23-1-00	Widnes NFP Naughton Park L22-14 G: Watson; T: Coley 2, Craig
1-2-00	Waterhead (Oldham) CC3 Gigg Lane W74-1 G: Watson 5; T: Coussons 2, Craig 2, P Barrow 2, Henare 2, Casey, Roach, Highton, Smith, English, T Barrow, Coley, Bateman
6-2-00	Rochdale Hornets NFP Gigg Lane W34-16 G: Watson 9; T: Coussons, P Barrow, Craig, Roach
13-2-00	St Helens CC4 Gigg Lane L22-36 G: Watson 2, Loughlin; T: Coley, Casey, Bateman, Coussons
20-2-00	Batley NFP Gigg Lane L16-32 G: Watson 2; T: Craig, Smith, Nanyn
5-3-00	Whitehaven NFP Recreation Ground W16-20 G: Nanyn 2; T: Craig, Coussons, Smith Roach
12-3-00	Barrow NFP Gigg Lane W35-22 G: Nanyn 3, Casey 1dg; T: Billy 3, Casey, Roach, Smith, Coussons
19-3-00	Hull KR NFP New Craven Park L54-16 G: Nanyn 2; T: Smith, Randall, Bateman
26-3-00	Keighley NFP Gigg Lane L12-34 G: Watson 2; T: Craig, Watson
2-4-00	Doncaster NFP Belle Vue L28-14 G: Watson 2 Nanyn; T: Smith, Henare
9-4-00	Dewsbury NFP Gigg Lane D14-14 G: Watson 1 + 2dg, Nanyn; T: Coussons, Craig
16-4-00	Sheffield Eagles NFP Gigg Lane W38-30 G: Watson 5; T: Henare 2, English, Coussons, Watson, Roach, Nanyn
21-4-00	Workington Town NFP Gigg Lane W38-34 G: Watson 3, Nanyn 2; T: English, Billy, Henare, Coussons, Furey, Roach, Pickavance
24-4-00	Oldham NFP Boundary Park L34-28 G: Watson 4; T: Roach 2, Smith, Watson, Billy
1-5-00	Featherstone Rovers NFP Post Office Road L28-14 G: Watson; T: Loughlin, Coussons, Henare
7-5-00	Hunslet NFP Gigg Lane L24-31 G: Watson 2; T: Roach 2, English, Coussons, Smith
10-5-00	York NFP Huntington Stadium W14-30 G: Watson 5; T: Coussons 2, Cushion, Loughlin, Henare
14-5-00	Leigh NFP Gigg Lane L12-46 G: Watson 2; T: Roach, Coussons
21-5-00	Lancashire Lynx NFP Victory Park W6-68 G: Watson 8; T: S. Barrow 2, Craig 2, Nanyn 2, Knowles, Roach, Furey, Coussons, Smith, Billy, Henare
26-5-00	Widnes NFP Gigg Lane L12-28 G: Watson 2; T: Watson, Roach
29-5-00	Rochdale Hornets NFP Spotland Stadium W21-32 G: Watson 2, Nanyn 2; T: Smith 2, Randall, Nanyn, Billy, Knowles
4-6-00	Batley NFP Mount Pleasant W24-28 G: Watson 2; T: Craig 2, Nanyn 2, Billy, Roach
9-6-00	Whitehaven NFP Edge Hall Road (home) D28-28 G: Nanyn 4; T: Randall 2, Smith, Craig, Casey
18-6-00	Barrow NFP Craven Park L34-22 G: Craig 2, Nanyn; T: Randall, Craig, Bateman, Nanyn
25-6-00	York NFP Gigg Lane W50-12 G: Watson 7; T: Henare, Casey, Billy, Craig, Coussons, Roach, English, Loughlin, Cushion
2-7-00	Keighley NFP Lawkholme Lane L66-12 G: Watson 2; T: Henare, Smith

Season 2001

3-12-00	Chorley Lynx NFP Victory Park W 12-30 G: Nanyn 3; T: Nanyn, 2, P Loughlin, Smith, Cheetham, Crossland
10-12-00	Whitehaven NFP Recreation Ground W4-8 T: Cheetham, Smith
17-12-00	Barrow NFP Gigg Lane W26-24 G: Nanyn 3; T: Russell, English, Nanyn, Mead, Smith
2-1-01	Leigh NFP Hilton Park L46-4 T: Cushion
7-1-01	Rochdale Hornets NFP Gigg Lane L4-8 T: Nanyn
15-1-01	Widnes NFP Naughton Park L16-8 G: Nanyn 2; T: Bateman
28-1-01	New Earswick (York) CC3 Gigg Lane W44-12 G: Nanyn 4; T: Nanyn 2, Stazicker 2, Cheetham 2, Napolitano, Bateman, Peet
4-2-01	Workington Town NFP Gigg Lane L20-29 G: P Loughlin, Nanyn; T: Veivers, Smith, Hudson, Cheetham
11-2-01	Leeds CC4 Gigg Lane L10-106 G: Nanyn; T: P. Loughlin, Smith
18-2-01	Hunslet NFP South Leeds Stadium L26-16 G: Nanyn 2; T: P. Loughlin 2, Nanyn
4-3-01	Dewsbury NFP Gigg Lane L18-20 G: Nanyn 3; T: Smith 2, Veivers
11-3-01	Hull KR NFP New Craven Park L32-6 G: Nanyn; T: Doherty
18-3-01	Featherstone Rovers NFP Gigg Lane W28-25 G: Nanyn 4; T: Hudson 2, Nanyn, Barraclough, Mead
25-3-01	York NFP Gigg Lane W74-0 G: Nanyn 9; T: Nanyn 3, Veivers 2, Hudson 2, Smith 2, Holdstock 2, Furey, Evans, Bateman
1-4-01	Batley NFP Gigg Lane L12-34 G: Nanyn 2; T: Bateman 2
8-4-01	Sheffield Eagles NFP Gigg Lane L22-23 G: Nanyn 3; T: Smith 2, Nanyn, Napolitano
13-4-01	Keighley NFP Lawkholme Lane W22-26 G: Nanyn 4, Waring 2dg; T: Smith, Cushion, Cheetham, Bateman
15-4-01	Leigh NFP Gigg Lane L0-40
22-4-01	Doncaster NFP Gigg Lane W19-18 G: Nanyn, Evans 1dg; T: Napolitano, Nanyn, Bateman, Russell
2-5-01	Oldham NFP Gigg Lane L10-33 G: Nanyn; T: Furey, Waring
5-5-01	Gateshead Thunder NFP Gigg Lane W20-8 G: Nanyn 2; T: Cheetham 2, Smith, Doherty
9-5-01	Oldham NFP Boundary Park L22-20 G: Nanyn 4; T: Mead, Doherty, Cheetham
13-5-01	Doncaster NFP Belle Vue L27-26 G: Nanyn 5; T: Smith 2, Doherty, Gallagher
20-5-01	Barrow NFP Craven Park L40-26 G: Nanyn 3; T: English, Bateman, Waring, Barraclough, Smith
27-5-01	Rochdale Hornets NFP Spotland Stadium L32-9 G: Nanyn 2, Waring dg; T: Holdstock
3-6-01	Widnes NFP Gigg Lane L0-62
10-6-01	Batley NFP Mount Pleasant L38-24 G: Nanyn 2; T: Bateman 2, Chambers, Evans, Nanyn
17-6-01	Workington Town NFP Derwent Park L34-10 G: Nanyn; T: Woods, Gallagher
24-6-01	Hunslet NFP Willows (home) W30-20 G: Nanyn 2, Doherty; T: Woods 2, Chambers, Bateman, Doherty, Mead
1-7-01	Dewsbury NFP New Crown Flatt W16-42 G: Nanyn 7; T: English 2, Woods, Veivers, Nanyn, Evans, Butler

Season 2002

9-12-01	Hull KR NFP Gigg Lane L 6-28 G: Nanyn; T: Dickinson
16-12-01	Rochdale Hornets NFP Spotland Stadium L22-10 G: Wingfield; T: Roach, Nanyn
13-1-02	Chorley Lynx NFP Victory Park L24-14 G: Nanyn 3; T: Dean, Fitzpatrick
20-1-02	Workington Town NFP Gigg Lane L6-41 G: Nanyn; T: Roach
30-1-02	Skirlaugh (Hull) CC3 Gigg Lane W32-24 AET G: Nanyn 4; T: Nanyn 2, Fitzpatrick, Shea, Woods, Roach
10-2-02	Widnes CC4 Gigg Lane L0-54
17-2-02	Huddersfield NFP Gigg Lane L4-48 T: Woods
24-2-02	Dewsbury NFP Gigg Lane L12-75 G: Nanyn, Wingfield; T: Woods, Barraclough
3-3-02	Doncaster NFP Belle Vue L40-14 G: Russell 2, Wingfield; T: Dean 2
10-3-02	Sheffield Eagles NFP Gigg Lane L8-14 G: Russell 2; T: Barraclough
17-3-02	Featherstone Rovers NFP Post Office Road L64-6 G: Russell; T: Fitzpatrick
24-3-02	Keighley NFP Gigg Lane W33-6 G: Russell 3, Wingfield, Fitzpatrick dg; T: Thorpe 2, Shea, Fitzpatrick, Barraclough, Russell
29-3-02	Leigh NC-W Hilton Park L60-4 T: Roach
7-4-02	Barrow NC-W Craven Park L68-18 G: Nanyn 3; T: Nanyn, Mead, Wingfield
14-4-02	Chorley Lynx NC-W Gigg Lane L22-28 G: Nanyn 3; T: Fitzpatrick 2, Nanyn, Thorpe
21-4-02	Workington Town NC-W Derwent Park L54-6 G: Nanyn; T: Barraclough
5-5-02	Whitehaven NC-W Hilton Park (home) W29-20 G: Nanyn 4, Dean 1dg; T: Thorpe, Mead, English, Nanyn, Hansen
26-5-02	Leigh NFP Hilton Park (home) L6-40 G: Nanyn; T: Barraclough
2-6-02	Whitehaven NFP Recreation Ground W26-34 G: Dean 5; T: Roach 2, Cannon, Barraclough, Hudson, Thorpe
9-6-02	Barrow NFP Craven Park L48-4 T: Roach
16-6-02	Batley NFP Mount Pleasant L34-16 G: Nanyn 2; T: Russell 2, Hudson
21-6-02	Hunslet NFP Hilton Park (home) D24-24 G: Nanyn 4; T: Mead 2, Johnson, Dean
5-7-02	Barrow NFP Hilton Park (home) L14-25 G: Nanyn; T: Thorpe, Nanyn, English
14-7-02	Gateshead Thunder NFP International Stadium W24-38 G: Nanyn 5; T: Hudson 2, English 2, Gibbons, Cushion, Dean
17-7-02	Oldham NFP Hurst Cross, Ashton L46-8 T: Nanyn, Stenhouse
21-7-02	Huddersfield NFP McAlpine Stadium L54-14 G: Nanyn 3; T: Holdstock, English
28-7-02	Featherstone Rovers NFP Victory Park (home) L24-40 G: Nanyn 2; T: Johnson 2, Holdstock 2, Ellison
4-8-02	Doncaster NFP Moor Lane L12-29 G: Nanyn 2; T: Holdstock, Stenhouse
11-8-02	Keighley NFP Lawkholme Lane L28-18 G: Nanyn; T: Cushion, Johnson, Stenhouse, Hudson
18-8-02	Chorley Lynx NFP Moor Lane W43-0 G: Nanyn 5, Dean 1dg; T: Stenhouse 3, Nanyn 2, Hudson 2, Ellison
25-8-02	Sheffield Eagles NFP Don Valley Stadium L24-21 G: Nanyn 4, Dean 1dg; T: Dean, Nanyn, Mahoney
28-8-02	Gateshead Thunder NFP Moor Lane W30-24 G: Nanyn 3; T: Roach 3, Russell, Johnson, Nanyn
1-9-02	Leigh NFP Hilton Park L60-14 G: Nanyn; T: Nanyn 2, Hudson
8-9-02	Whitehaven NFP Moor Lane W40-30 G: Nanyn 6; T: Johnson 2, Stenhouse, Hudson, Ellison, Nanyn, Roach
20-9-02	Sheffield Eagles NL1QS-EPO Don Valley Stadium L30-20 G: Nanyn, Wingfield; T: Gallagher, Cushion, Hansen, Stenhouse

Season 2003

19-01-03	Salford NLC Willows L 6-58 G: Hough; T: Wingfield
26-1-03	Shaw Cross (Dewsbury) CC3 Moor Lane W46-0 G: Hough 5; T: Thorpe 3, Cannon 3, English, Smith, Cheetham
2-2-03	Leigh NLC Moor Lane L10-24 G: Smith; T: Wingfield, Thorpe
9-2-03	Chorley Lynx CC4 Victory Park W16-32 G: Wingfield 4; T: Tassell 3, Ellison, Thorpe, Hudson
23-2-03	Oldham NLC Moor Lane L16-24 G: Hough 2; T: Barraclough, Roach, Cannon
2-3-03	Featherstone Rovers CC5 Moor Lane W32-10 G: Hough 3+2dg; T: Hassan, English, Johnson, Thorpe, Knox, Cushion
9-3-03	Whitehaven NLC Recreation Ground L38-6 G: Wingfield; T: Bithel
16-3-03	Wigan CCQF JJB Stadium (switched) L12-70 G: Hough 2; T: Russell, Leatham
19-3-03	Rochdale Hornets NLC Spotland Stadium L24-14 G: Hough 3; T: Hough, Bithel
23-3-03	Leigh NLC Hilton Park L62-6 G: Hough; T: Hassan
30-3-03	Rochdale Hornets NLC Moor Lane W26-22 G: Hough 3; T: Roach, Hudson, Hough, Ellison, Cannon
2-4-03	Salford NLC Moor Lane L0-72
6-4-03	Oldham NLC Boundary Park L68-14 G: Russell; T: Mead, Hudson, Russell
13-4-03	Whitehaven NLC Moor Lane D22-22 G: Hough 3; T: Hudson 2, Knox, Ellison
18-4-03	Chorley Lynx NL2 Moor Lane W31-12 G: Hough 5+1dg; T: Roach, Hudson, Smith, Tassell, Hough
21-4-03	Workington Town NL2 Derwent Park L8-4 T: Loughlin
4-5-03	Gateshead Thunder NL2 Moor Lane L35-38 G: Hough 4+1dg, Wingfield; T: Roach 2, Cheetham 2, Wingfield, English
9-5-03	Sheffield Eagles NL2 Don Valley Stadium W18-23 G: Hough 5+1dg; T: English, Cheetham, Loughlin
1-6-03	York NL2 Huntington Stadium L40-2 G: Hough
8-6-03	London Skolars NL2 New River Stadium W8-31 G: Hough 5+1dg; T: Knox, Roach, Ellison, Cannon
15-6-03	Barrow NL2 Craven Park L42-20 G: Russell, Hough; T: Roach, Hough, Tassell, Hassan
22-6-03	Hunslet NL2 Moor Lane D10-10 G: Hough 2+2dg; T: Ellison
29-6-03	Keighley NL2 Lawkholme Lane L18-15 G: Hough 1+1dg; T: Tassell 2, Knox
13-7-03	Sheffield Eagles NL2 Moor Lane W20-18 G: Hough 4; T: Cannon, Hudson, Roach
20-7-03	Gateshead Thunder NL2 International Stadium W30-39 G: Hough 7, Patel 1dg; T: Hudson 3, Roach 2, Ellison
27-7-03	Workington Town NL2 Moor Lane W56-12 G: Hough 8, Gallagher 2; T: Bithel 2, Thorpe, Tassell, Roach, Patel, English, Roe, Loughlin
3-8-03	Chorley Lynx NL2 Victory Park L41-22 G: Hough 5; T: Lomax, Thorpe, English
10-8-03	London Skolars NL2 Moor Lane W34-12 G: Hough 4, Gallagher; T: Bithel, Gallagher, Knox, Roach, Hough, English
17-8-03	York NL2 Moor Lane W38-16 G: Hough 4+2dg; T: Roach 3, Hudson 2, Tassell, Loughlin,
24-8-03	Hunslet NL2 South Leeds Stadium L46-14 G: Hough 3; T: Gorski, Thorpe
31-8-03	Keighley NL2 Moor Lane L17-19 G: Hough 2+1dg; T: Cannon, Tassell, Roach
7-9-03	Barrow NL2 Moor Lane L34-38 G: Hough 2, Russell; T: Barton, Bithel, Barraclough, Roach, Hudson, Tassell, Hough

Season 2004

1-2-04	Leigh NLC Park Lane L6-22 G: Ashton; T: Maye
8-2-04	East Hull CC3 Park Lane L14-26 G: Ashton; T: Irwin, Ashton, Maye
15-2-04	Whitehaven NLC Recreation Ground L38-10 G: Ashton; T: English, Ayres
22-2-04	Oldham NLC Park Lane L18-30 G: Ayres; T: Cushion 2, English, Llewellyn
7-3-04	Chorley Lynx NLC Park Lane W27-24 G: Maye, Ashton 2, Ayres 1dg; T: Roach, Irwin, Cannon, Bolton, Maye
21-3-04	Leigh NLC Hilton Park L66-6 G: Wingfield; T: Heaton
28-3-04	Whitehaven NLC Park Lane L6-34 G: Maye; T: Irwin
4-4-04	Oldham NLC Boundary Park L42-15 G: Maye, Ashton 2+1dg; T: Ayres, Cannon
9-4-04	Chorley Lynx NLC Victory Park L20-12 G: Ayres 2; T: Roach, Ayres
12-4-04	Gateshead Thunder NL2 Park Lane W42-10 G: Ayres 4, Ashton; T: Maye 2, Bolton 2, Sinfield, Cannon, English, Patel
19-4-04	Dewsbury NL2 New Crown Flatt W8-35 G: Ayres 5+1dg; T: Cannon 2, Maye 2, Wingfield, Thorpe
2-5-04	Workington Town NL2 Park lane W64-26 G: Ayres 9, Smith; T: Ayres, Bolton, English 3, Smith, Maye 2, Roach, Cannon, Barraclough,
9-5-04	Hunslet NL2 South Leeds Stadium L42-20 G: Ayres 2; T: Sinfield, Thorpe, English, Irwin
23-5-04	Barrow NL2 Park Lane L10-46 G: Ayres; T: Cannon, Stazicker
30-5-04	York NL2 Huntington Stadium L44-24 G: Ayres 4; T: Cushion, Irwin, English, Cannon
13-6-04	London Skolars NL2 New River Stadium L28-26 G: Ayres 3; T: Cannon 2, Maye, Llewellyn, Irwin
20-6-04	Chorley Lynx NL2 Park Lane W28-20 G: Ashton 5; T: Hodson, Sinfield, English, Maye
4-7-04	Sheffield Eagles NL2 Don Valley Stadium W16-32 G: Ashton 6; T: Maye, Smith, Russell, Irwin, Cannon
11-7-04	Dewsbury Nl2 Park Lane W34-15 G: Ashton 5; T: Rogers, Ashton, Roach 2, Irwin, Thorpe
25-7-04	Workington Town NL2 Derwent Park L40-22 G: Ayres 3; T: Russell, Maye, Thorpe, Smith
1-8-04	Hunslet NL2 Park Lane W33-16 G: Ashton 2, Ayres 2, Coates 1dg; T: Roach, Cannon, Hodson, English 2, Tyrell
9-8-04	Barrow NL2 Craven Park W12-22 G: Ashton 3; T: English, Patel, Maye, Llewellyn
15-8-04	York NL2 Park Lane L12-48 G: Ashton 4; T: English
22-8-04	London Skolars Nl2 Park Lane W42-12 G: Ayres, Smith 4; T: Russell, Maye, Coates, English, Gardner, Hodson, Thorpe, Roach
29-8-04	Chorley Lynx NL2 Victory Park W30-43 G: Smith 2, Russell 3, Patel 1dg; T: Cushion, Maye 2, English, Hodson, Thorpe, Russell, Whittaker
5-9-04	Sheffield Eagles NL2 Park Lane W32-24 G: Russell 4; T: Thorpe, Patel, Smith, Maye 2, Cushion
12-9-04	Gateshead Thunder NL2 International Stadium W23-28 G: Russell 2; T: Smith, Maye 2, English, Llewellyn, Sinfield
19-9-04	Workington Town NL1 QS-EPO Park Lane L38-44 G: Ashton 4, Russell; T: English, Ayres, Llewellyn, Hodson 2, Thorpe, Coates

Season 2005

13-02-05	Rochdale Hornets NLC Park Lane W 20-14 G: Marsh 2; T: Maye, Marsh 2, English
18-2-05	Blackpool Panthers NLC Bloomfield Road W24-34 G: Marsh 5; T: Joseph, Maye 2, Billy 2, Oldham
27-2-05	Oldham NLC Park Lane W46-14 G: Marsh 7; T: Marsh, Heaton, English 3, Sinfield, Rogers, Watson
6-3-05	Oldham NLC Boundary Park W30-37 G: Watson 3, Marsh 1+1dg; T: English 2, Billy, Heaton, Patterson, Sinfield, Joseph
13-3-05	Locomotiv Moscow CC3 Park Lane W70-10 G: Marsh 9; T: Maye 4, Marsh, Joseph, Russell, Patterson 2, Billy 2, Oldham, Watson
20-3-05	Rochdale Hornets NLC Spotland Stadium L54-20 -; T: Patterson, Irwin 2, Patel, Maye
25-3-05	Blackpool Panthers NLC Park Lane D14-14 G: Marsh; T: Irwin, Coates, Maye
28-3-05	York NL2 Huntington Stadium W18-34 G: Marsh 5; T: Marsh, English, Patterson, Gardner, Coates, Maye
3-4-05	Widnes CC4 Naughton Park L32-18 G: Marsh 3; T: Billy 2, Joseph
10-4-05	Workington Town NL2 Park Lane W56-18 G: Marsh 8; T: English 3, Joseph, Sou, Coates 2, Patterson 2, Billy
17-4-05	Dewsbury NL2 New Crown Flatt L48-10 G: Marsh; T: Heaton 2
24-4-05	London Skolars NL2 New River Stadium W8-38 G: Marsh 3; T: Marsh 2, Billy 3, English, Patterson, Russell
1-5-05	Batley NLCQPO Park Lane W40-24 G: Marsh 2, Smith 2; T: Patterson 3, Sinfield, Heaton 2, Billy, Maye
15-5-05	Blackpool Panthers NL2 Park Lane W84-12 G: Marsh 9, Joseph; T: English 2, Patterson 3, Billy 2, Marsh 2, Coates, Oldham 2, Southern, Parry, Rogers, Ayres
22-5-05	Keighley NL2 Lawkholme Lane W12-30 G: Marsh 5; T: Coates 2, Marsh, Irwin, English
29-5-05	Hull KR NLCQF New Craven Park L62-0
5-6-05	Hunslet NL2 South Leeds Stadium L30-20 G: Coates 2; T: Billy, Irwin, English, Patterson
12-6-05	Gateshead Thunder NL2 Park Lane L32-57 G: Coates, Ayres; T: Billy, Heaton, Leigh, Joseph, Patterson, Coates, Irwin
26-6-05	Sheffield Eagles NL2 Park Lane W42-24 G: Marsh 7; T: Patterson 2, English, Watson 2, Oldham, Sinfield
3-7-05	Workington Town NL2 Derwent Park L23-20 G: Marsh 2; T: Marsh, Joseph, Maye, English
10-7-05	York NL2 Park Lane L16-32 G: Marsh 2; T: Maye, Marsh, English
24-7-05	Blackpool Panthers NL2 Bloomfield Road W26-51 G: Marsh 7+1dg; T: Billy 3, Joseph, Maye, Parry, English 2, Marsh
31-7-05	London Skolars NL2 Park Lane W44-12 G: Marsh 6; T: Maye, Billy 2, English, Heaton 2, Smith, Patel
7-8-05	Hunslet NL2 Park Lane W34-20 G: Marsh 3; T: Patterson, English 2, Billy, Oldham, Marsh, Maye
14-8-05	Gateshead Thunder NL2 International Stadium L58-10 G: Marsh; T: Farrimond, Billy
21-8-05	Keighley NL2 Park Lane W46-0 G: Marsh 7; T: Joseph 2, Oldham, Marsh 2, English, Heaton 2
2-9-05	Sheffield Eagles NL2 Don Valley Stadium W14-38 G: Marsh 5; T: Billy 2, Joseph, Llewellyn, Parry, Marsh, Patterson
11-9-05	Dewsbury NL2 Park Lane L18-22 G: Marsh 3; T: Marsh 2, Parry
18-9-05	Hunslet NL1 QS-EPO Park Lane W40-28 G: Marsh 6; T: Maye, Parry, Marsh, Heaton, Crabtree, Patterson, English
25-9-05	Workington Town NL1 QS-ESF Derwent Park L17-16 G: Marsh 4; T: Billy, Llewellyn

Season 2006

12-02-06	Widnes NLC Naughton Park L10-18 G: McGovern; T: Billy, Parry
19-2-06	Blackpool Panthers NLC Park Lane W42-10 G: Smith 3, McGovern 2; T: Smith, Ashton 2, Billy, Coates 2, Moana, Oldham
26-2-06	Leigh NLC Park Lane L20-30 G: Watson, Smith; T: Watson, Moana 2, Oldham
5-3-06	Blackpool Panthers NLC Bloomfield Road W16-26 G: McGovern 3, Watson 2; T: Coates, English 2, Farrimond
14-3-06	Sheffield Eagles CC3 Park Lane W42-18 G: Smith 5; T: English 3, Ashton 2, Saywell 2, Billy
19-3-06	Widnes NLC Park Lane L16-64 G: Watson 2; T: Saywell, Moana 2
26-3-06	Leigh NLC Hilton Park W14-18 G: Smith 3; T: Saywell, Stout, English
2-4-06	York CC4 Park Lane L18-20 G: Smith, McGovern 2; T: Saywell, Billy 2
9-4-06	Barrow NL2 Park Lane W22-20 G: McGovern; T: Moana, Sinfield, Marshall, Morley, Alstead
14-4-06	Blackpool Panthers NL2 Park Lane W56-24 G: McGovern 2, Smith 6; T: Saywell 2, Watson, Moana, Billy, Stout, English, Morley, Alstead 2
17-4-06	London Skolars NL2 New River Stadium W24-38 G: Smith 3, McGovern 2; T: Saywell, Morley, Ashton, Watson, Moana 2, Stout
23-4-06	Workington Town NLCQFQ Derwent Park L46-30 G: Crabtree 4, Coates; T: Moana 2, Ashton, D Woods 2
30-4-06	Gateshead Thunder NL2 Park Lane W26-21 G: Marsh 5; T: Alstead, D Woods 2, Marsh
10-5-06	Workington Town NL2 Derwent Park L23-18 G: Marsh 3; T: D. Woods, Billy, English
14-5-06	Barrow NL2 Craven Park W12-16 G: Marsh 2; T: Ashton, Billy, Alstead
21-5-06	Dewsbury NL2 Park Lane L18-22 G: Marsh; T: Saywell 2, Stout, Smith
26-5-06	Blackpool Panthers NL2 Bloomfield Road W8-44 G: Marsh 6; T: Llewellyn, Moana, Sinfield, Parry, Saywell 2, Stout, Marsh
2-6-06	Hunslet NL2 Willows (home) W54-22 G: McGovern 7; T: Moana 2, Saywell 3, English 2, McGovern, Llewellyn, Sinfield
11-6-06	Celtic Crusaders NL2 Park Lane L18-50 G: McGovern 3; T: Billy 2, Morley
18-6-06	Featherstone Rovers NL2 Post Office Road L27-24 G: Smith, McGovern 3; T: Ashton 2, Smith, P. Wood
25-6-06	Workington Town NL2 Park Lane W46-30 G: Marsh 7; T: Alstead, P. Wood 4, English, Patel, Billy
2-7-06	Celtic Crusaders NL2 Brewery Field W10-21 G: Marsh 4+1dg; T: Marsh, Moana, Saywell
9-7-06	Sheffield Eagles NL2 Park Lane L14-24 G: Marsh 3; T: P. Wood, English
16-7-06	Featherstone Rovers NL2 Park Lane W26-22 G: Marsh 3; T: Johnson, Stout, Sinfield, Marsh, P. Wood
28-7-06	Sheffield Eagles NL2 Don Valley Stadium L18-14 G: Marsh; T: D. Woods, Saywell, Sinfield
2-8-06	Hunslet NL2 South Leeds Stadium D24-24 G: Marsh, Hough; T: Wakelin, Johnson, D. Woods 2, Moana
6-08-06	Keighley NL2 Lawkholme Lane L28-6 G: Marsh; T: McGovern
13-8-06	London Skolars NL2 Park Lane W58-12 G: McGovern 9; T: McCurrie, Saywell 3, Hough 2, English, Moana, Stout, D. Woods
20-8-06	Dewsbury NL2 New Crown Flatt L20-12 G: McGovern, Hough; T: D. Woods, Moana
3-9-06	Keighley NL2 Park Lane W54-10 G: Hough 7; T: Johnson 2, Moana, Saywell 3, Marsh, Hough 2, Alstead
10-9-06	Gateshead Thunder NL2 International Stadium W24-32 G: Marsh 3, Hough; T: D. Woods 2, Alcock 2, English, Johnson
17-9-06	Barrow EPO Park Lane W26-20 G: Hough 5; T: D. Woods 2, Billy, McCurrie
24-9-06	Featherstone Rovers ESF Post Office Road W14-27 G: Hough 3, Marsh dg; T: Alcock, Saywell 2, D. Woods, Smith
1-10-06	Celtic Crusaders FE Brewery Field W26-27 AET+GP G: Hough, Marsh, McGovern; T: Alcock, D. Woods, Marsh 2, McGovern; Golden point: Hough 1dg
8-10-06	Sheffield Eagles GF Halliwell-Jones Stadium L35-10 G: McGovern; T: Saywell, Alstead

Season 2007

11-02-07	Hunslet NLC Park Lane W 38-20 G: McGovern 5; T: Newton 2, Morley, Line, English, Saywell, Walker
18-2-07	Oldham NLC Boundary Park W18-28 G: McGovern, Hough; T: D. Woods 4, P. Wood, Saywell
25-2-07	Rochdale Hornets NLC Park Lane L14-40 G: Ashall; T: Billy 2, Brocklehurst
4-3-07	Hunslet NLC South Leeds Stadium D10-10 G: McGovern; T: Walker, D. Woods
11-3-07	Locomotiv Moscow CC3 Park Lane W60-20 G: McGovern 8; T: Saywell 3, Ashall 2, P. Wood, D. Woods 2, English, Johnson, McGovern
18-3-07	Rochdale Hornets NLC Spotland Stadium L42-10 G: McGovern; T: P. Wood, Ashton
25-3-07	Oldham NLC Park Lane L18-42 G: McGovern 3; T: Saywell 2, English
1-4-07	Barrow CC4 Park Lane L14-47 G: McGovern D. Woods, Morley, Smith
6-4-07	Blackpool Panthers NL2 Memorial Ground W34-40 G: McGovern, Marsh 3; T: Williams 3, P. Wood, Line, Saywell, Moana, McGovern
9-4-07	Barrow NL2 Park Lane L30-35 G: Marsh 5; T: Saywell, English 2, Alcock, Hayes
15-4-07	London Skolars NL2 Park Lane W34-26 G: Marsh 3; T: Billy, Johnson, Williams 3, Brocklehurst, D. Woods
22-4-07	Rochdale Hornets NLCQFQ Spotland Stadium L30-16 G: Ogden 2; T: Billy, P. Wood, Moana
28-4-07	Celtic Crusaders NL2 Brewery Field L82-4 T: Johnson
7-5-07	Gateshead Thunder NL2 Park Lane W58-12 G: Marsh 9; T: Line, D. Woods 3, Billy 2, Moana, Ogden, Williamson, P Wood
20-5-07	York NL2 Park Lane L26-38 G: Marsh 3; T: Alcock, Billy, Williams, Marsh, Watkins
27-5-07	Featherstone Rovers NL2 Post Office Road L42-4 T: Gorton
3-6-07	Barrow NL2 Craven Park L52-24 G: Hough 2; T: Johnson, Morley, Saywell 2, Ashall
10-6-07	Hunslet NL2 South Leeds Stadium W10-17 G: McGovern 4+1dg; T: Bates, Billy
17-6-07	Keighley NL2 Park Lane W44-18 G: McGovern 6; T: McGovern, Gorton, Line, Saywell, Hough, Ashton, Hull, Marsh
24-6-07	London Skolars NL2 New River Stadium L34-12 G: Marsh 2; T: Ashall, Bates
1-7-07	Workington Town NL2 Derwent Park L38-33 G: McGovern 6+1dg; T: Gorton, Hayes, Moana, Smith, P. Wood
8-7-07	Oldham NL2 Park Lane W17-10 G: McGovern 2+1dg; T: English, Saywell, Ashall
15-7-07	Celtic Crusaders NL2 Park Lane L20-26 G: Marsh 2; T: Gorton, Smith, Saywell, Hough
21-7-07	Gateshead Thunder NL2 International Stadium W8-34 G: Marsh 5; T: Hull 2, Bates, P. Wood, Marsh, Alcock
29-7-07	Keighley NL2 Lawkholme Lane L52-22 G: Marsh 3; T: Moana, Hull, Marsh, Billy
5-8-07	Featherstone Rovers NL2 Park Lane L22-28 G: Marsh, McGovern 2; T: Saywell 2, Gorton, Duffy
12-8-07	Blackpool Panthers NL2 Park Lane W70-20 G: Marsh 9, McGovern 2; T: Billy, Bates, English 2, Brocklehurst, Alcock, Line 2, P. Wood 2, Saywell 2
19-8-07	York NL2 Huntington Stadium W16-22 G: Marsh 5; T: Moana, Marsh, Saywell
2-9-07	Hunslet NL2 Park Lane W14-12 G: Marsh; T: Moana 2, Brocklehurst
5-9-07	Oldham NL2 Boundary Park L30-22 G: Marsh 3; T: P. Wood, Duffy, Marsh 2
9-9-07	Workington Town NL2 Park Lane W36-26 G: Marsh 6; T: Saywell 2, Moana 2, Billy 2
16-9-07	Oldham EPO Boundary Park L36-6 G: Marsh; T: Ashall

Season 2008

01-02-08	Oldham NRC Boundary Park L20-22 G: Hawkyard 4; T: Billy, Ball, Johnson
10-02-08	Rochdale Hornets NRC Park Lane L34-36 G: Hawkyard 5; T: Bamford, Hull, Billy 2, Hulse, McGovern
17-02-08	Salford NRC Park Lane L8-48 T: Saywell 2
24-02-08	Rochdale Hornets NRC Spotland Stadium W38-34 G: Hawkyard 5; T: Saywell, Billy, McGovern, Gibson 2, Moana 2
29-02-08	Salford NRC Willows L6-70 G: Hawkyard; T: Brand
09-03-08	Wath Brow CC3 Recreation Ground (Whitehaven) W40-14 G: Hawkyard 6; T: Bamford 2, Billy, 2 Hawkyard, Wood, Hull
16-03-08	Oldham NRC Park Lane L10-52 G: Hawkyard; T: Sykes, Ball
21-03-08	Blackpool Panthers NL2 Park Lane W 44-30 G: Hawkyard, McGovern 5; T: Gorton, Billy 3, Line, Moana, McGovern, Hull
24-03-08	Keighley NL2 Cougar Park L12-21 G: McGovern 2; T: Saywell 2
30-03-08	Doncaster NL2 Keepmoat Stadium L18-36 G: Sykes 3; T: Wood, Moana, Johnson
13-04-08	London Skolars NL2 Park Lane W34-24 G: Bamford 2, Sykes 2, Brand; T: English 2, Saywell, Gorton, Johnson, Gibson
20-04-08	Oldham CC4 Park Lane L 8-20 -; T: Hamilton, Bamford
27-04-08	Workington Town NL2 Derwent Park W 30-20 G: Brand 5; T: Hamilton, Brand, Gorton, Billy, Wood
05-05-08	Gateshead Thunder NL2 Park Lane L 20-36 G: Brand 2; T: Frodsham 2, Billy, Hayes
11-05-08	York NL2 Park Lane L 28-50 G: Hawkyard 4; T: Williamson, Billy, Hulse, Sykes, Hayes
18-05-08	Oldham NL2 Boundary Park L 20-30 G: Frodsham, Hawkyard; T: Billy 3, Hawkyard
25-05-08	Blackpool Panthers NL2 Memorial Ground L28-30 G: Hawkyard 3, McGovern; T: Hamilton, Billy, Moana 2, Hayes
01-06-08	Hunslet NL2 South Leeds Stadium W 17-6 G: Hawkyard 4, McGovern 1dg; T: Bamford, Ashall
08-06-08	Workington Town NL2 Park Lane W 33-24 G: Hawkyard 4, McGovern 1dg; T: Hulse, McGovern, Williamson, Sykes, Ashall 2
15-06-08	Rochdale Hornets NL2 Park Lane L 22-54 G: McGovern 3; T: Hawkyard, Moana, Rigby, Wood
22-06-08	Gateshead Thunder NL2 International Stadium L 12 -28 G: Hawkyard 2; T: Saywell, Hayes
28-06-08	Barrow NL2 Craven Park L 14-70 G: Crook; T: Hulse, Saywell, Donoghue
09-07-08	Doncaster NL2 Park Lane L 16-44 G: Crook 2; T: Gorton, Moana, McGovern
12-07-08	London Skolars NL2 New River Stadium L 22-26 G: Crook 3; T: Gorton, English, Line, Moana
20-07-08	Keighley NL2 Park Lane L 6-40 G: McGovern; T: Sykes
27-07-08	York NL2 Huntington Stadium L 12-66 G: Hawkyard 2; T: English, Billy
03-08-08	Hunslet NL2 Park Lane W 36-20 G: Hawkyard 2, McGovern 4; T: English, Gorton, Billy, McGovern, Moana, Bamford
10-08-08	Rochdale Hornets NL2 Spotland Stadium L 26-50 G: McGovern 3; T: Hull, Rigby, Moana, Hulse, Bates
17-08-08	Oldham NL2 Park Lane L 20-38 G: McGovern 2; T: McGovern, Saywell, Hull 2
23-08-08	Barrow NL2 Park Lane L 12-31 G: Hawkyard 2; T: English, Gorton

Appendix D: Swinton Lions player-by-player from 1999 to 2008

Season 1999

Player	Appearances	Tries	Goals	Drop-Goals	Points
Steve Allison	(1)	0	0	0	0
Simon Ashcroft	13(3)	7	0	0	28
Paul Barrow	21(1)	6	0	0	24
Tony Barrow	14(5)	0	0	0	0
Matt Bateman	12(1)	4	0	0	16
Marlon Billy	21(2)	5	0	0	20
Ian Blease	17(9)	1	0	0	4
Sean Casey	24	8	0	3	35
Damien Cleary	12(3)	5	0	0	20
Andy Coley	2	0	0	0	0
Phil Cushion	17(10)	2	0	0	8
Cliff Eccles	23(2)	4	0	0	16
Jim Evans	20(5)	5	0	0	20
Richie Eyres	7(4)	3	0	0	12
Paul Gartland	6	2	0	0	8
Steve Gartland	16(11)	6	46	1	117
Martin Gleeson	(1)	0	0	0	0
Richard Henare	17(1)	11	0	0	44
Howard Hill	22(4)	6	0	0	24
Jason Hunter	6	1	0	0	4
Jake Johnson	(1)	2	0	0	8
Gerrard Killeen	1	0	0	0	0
Carl McCabe	18(1)	3	0	0	12
Dave McComas	1(1)	0	0	0	0
Mick Nanyn	3(1)	2	0	0	8
Gareth Norman	(1)	0	0	0	0
Gavin Price-Jones	13(3)	2	0	0	8
Wes Rogers	9(10)	3	0	0	12
Paul Smith	2(12)	3	0	0	12
Ryan Stazicker	3(6)	2	0	0	8
Paul Stevens	6	1	0	0	4
Steve Taylor	4(7)	2	0	0	8
Ian Watson	30	6	58	7	147
Mark Welsby	30	15	0	0	60
Darren Williams	(1)	0	0	0	0

Season 2000

Player	Appearances	Tries	Goals	Drop-Goals	Points
Paul Barrow	7(11)	3	0	0	12
Steve Barrow	3	2	0	0	8
Tony Barrow	8(19)	1	0	0	4
Matt Bateman	14(2)	6	0	0	24
Marlon Billy	25(3)	11	0	0	44
Sean Casey	17	5	0	2	22
Andy Coley	7(1)	7	0	0	28
Phil Coussons	28	18	0	0	72
Andy Craig	25(1)	16	2	0	68
Phil Cushion	6(12)	2	0	0	8
Wayne English	12(3)	5	0	0	20
Jim Evans	6(13)	0	0	0	0
Sean Fury	13(2)	2	0	0	8
Steve Gartland	2(2)	0	0	0	0
Richard Henare	9(8)	11	0	0	44
Chris Highton	20(1)	1	0	0	4
Matt Knowles	16(7)	2	0	0	8
Paul Loughlin	14(5)	7	1	0	20
Mick Nanyn	12(7)	8	18	0	68
Jonathan Neill	24(2)	0	0	0	0
Ian Pickavance	23(3)	3	0	0	12
Craig Randall	13(3)	5	0	0	20
Jason Roach	25(3)	16	0	0	64
Paul Smith	29	16	0	0	64
Ryan Stazicker	3(6)	0	0	0	0
Ian Watson	28	5	84	2	176
Mark Welsby	1(2)	0	0	0	0

Season 2001

Player	Appearances	Tries	Goals	Drop-Goals	Points
Rob Barraclough	29	2	0	0	8
Tony Barrow	2(5)	0	0	0	0
Matt Bateman	25	11	0	0	44
Danny Butler	1(17)	1	0	0	4
Nick Crammann	2(9)	0	0	0	0
Gareth Chambers	4	2	0	0	8
Andy Cheetham	14(4)	9	0	0	36
Paul Crossland	1(3)	1	0	0	4
Phil Cushion	22	2	0	0	8
Jon-Paul Doherty	15(9)	5	1	0	22
Wayne English	15(3)	4	0	0	16
Jim Evans	14(6)	3	0	1	13
Shaun Fury	15(2)	2	0	0	8
Rob Gallagher	5(4)	2	0	0	8
Lee Hansen	26(1)	0	0	0	0
Dale Holdstock	13(4)	3	0	0	12
Lee Hudson	11(3)	5	0	0	20
Wayne Jackman	1(1)	0	0	0	0
Dan Lewis	(5)	0	0	0	0
Mike Loughlin	7(4)	0	0	0	0
Paul Loughlin	10(1)	4	1	0	18
Adrian Mead	16(4)	4	0	0	16
Mick Nanyn	29	15	72	0	186
Carlo Napolitano	7(8)	3	0	0	12
Jonathan Neill	6	0	0	0	0
Chris Newall	4(5)	0	0	0	0
Kelvin Peet	7	1	0	0	4
Robert Russell	5(3)	2	0	0	8
Paul Smith	23(3)	16	0	0	64
Ryan Stazicker	5(8)	2	0	0	8
Phil Veivers	20(1)	5	0	0	20
Phil Waring	19(2)	2	0	3	11
Mike Woods	4	4	0	0	16

Season 2002

Player	Appearances	Tries	Goals	Drop-Goals	Points
Rob Baraclough	21	6	0	0	24
Danny Butler	3(12)	0	0	0	0
Peter Cannon	15	1	0	0	4
Gareth Chambers	3(6)	0	0	0	0
Andy Cheetham	(1)	0	0	0	0
Dean Conway	(1)	0	0	0	0
Phil Cushion	23(2)	3	0	0	12
Craig Dean	29(1)	6	5	3	37
Stuart Dickinson	7	1	0	0	4
Dave Ellison	7(3)	3	0	0	12
Wayne English	13(4)	5	0	0	20
Karl Fitzpatrick	16	6	0	1	25
Rob Gallagher	17(12)	1	0	0	4
Steve Gee	1	0	0	0	0
David Gibbons	13(2)	1	0	0	4
Lee Hansen	32(2)	2	0	0	8
Dale Holdstock	23(2)	4	0	0	16
Lee Hudson	16(4)	9	0	0	36
Adam Hughes	11(1)	0	0	0	0
Wayne Jackman	1	0	0	0	0
Jason Johnson	14	7	0	0	28
Andy Leathem	18(4)	0	0	0	0
Mike Loughlin	4(5)	0	0	0	0
Matt Mahoney	(5)	1	0	0	4
Adrian Mead	21(3)	4	0	0	16
Anthony Murray	2(1)	0	0	0	0
Mick Nanyn	27(2)	15	62	0	184
Jonathan Neill	(4)	0	0	0	0
Chris Newall	6(7)	0	0	0	0
Gareth Pratt	(4)	0	0	0	0
Jason Roach	17(5)	11	0	0	44
Robert Russell	13(5)	4	8	0	32
Peter Shaw	3(1)	0	0	0	0
Alan Shea	14(10)	2	0	0	8
Jamie Stenhouse	10(2)	8	0	0	32
Hugh Thorpe	26(3)	6	0	0	24
Mike Whiteside	11(2)	0	0	0	0
Craig Wingfield	7(20)	1	5	0	14
Mike Woods	11	3	0	0	12

Season 2003

Player	Appearances	Tries	Goals	Drop-Goals	Points
Mark Ashton	1(2)	0	0	0	0
Rob Baraclough	20(3)	2	0	0	8
Danny Barton	4	1	0	0	4
Grant Bithel	8(8)	6	0	0	24
Danny Butler	(2)	0	0	0	0
Peter Cannon	29	7	0	0	28
Andy Cheetham	8(7)	4	0	0	16
Phil Cushion	11(2)	1	0	0	4
Mick Durham	3(1)	0	0	0	0
Dave Ellison	18(3)	5	0	0	20
Wayne English	30	8	0	0	32
Rob Gallagher	13(2)	1	3	0	10
Andy Gorski	4	1	0	0	4
Lee Hansen	3(1)	0	0	0	0
Phil Hassan	21(2)	3	0	0	12
Chris Hough	28(1)	6	86	12	208
Lee Hudson	25(4)	13	0	0	52
Mark Hudspith	(1)	0	0	0	0
Jason Johnson	2(6)	1	0	0	4
Simon Knox	32	6	0	0	24
Andy Leathem	16	1	0	0	4
James Lomax	5(1)	1	0	0	4
Mike Loughlin	3(11)	4	0	0	16
Greg McAvoy	1	0	0	0	0
Adrian Mead	5(1)	1	0	0	4
David Ogden	(1)	0	0	0	0
Liam Owen	(2)	0	0	0	0
Safraz Patel	3(7)	1	0	1	5
Jason Roach	23(2)	17	0	0	68
Chris Roe	11(14)	1	0	0	4
Wes Rogers	2	0	0	0	0
Robert Russell	17(4)	2	3	0	14
Mike Saunders	3(1)	0	0	0	0
Alan Shea	3(4)	0	0	0	0
Kris Smith	7(10)	2	1	0	10
Kris Tassell	20(2)	12	0	0	48
Hugh Thorpe	19(5)	9	0	0	36
Danny Turner	(3)	0	0	0	0
Daniel Tyres	4(4)	0	0	0	0
Craig Wingfield	14(7)	3	6	0	24

Season 2004

Player	Appearances	Tries	Goals	Drop-Goals	Points
Paul Ashton	13(4)	2	37	1	83
Warren Ayres	21(6)	5	37	2	96
Rob Barraclough	2(3)	1	0	0	4
Grant Bithel	(2)	0	0	0	0
Mark Bolton	11(1)	4	0	0	16
Chris Brett	(3)	0	0	0	0
Peter Cannon	18(1)	12	0	0	48
Mick Coats	17(1)	2	0	1	9
Phil Cushion	19(1)	5	0	0	20
Wayne English	27	17	0	0	68
Lee Gardner	3(5)	1	0	0	4
Neil Hayden	4(2)	0	0	0	0
Danny Heaton	6(2)	1	0	0	4
Ian Hodson	23(2)	6	0	0	24
Chris Irwin	17(2)	8	0	0	32
Jake Johnstone	2(2)	0	0	0	0
Craig Kay	(1)	0	0	0	0
Alan Kilshaw	(1)	0	0	0	0
Tau Liku	7(8)	0	0	0	0
Dave Llewellyn	15(2)	5	0	0	20
Mike Loughlin	7(2)	0	0	0	0
Chris Maye	25	21	3	0	90
Safraz Patel	5(13)	3	0	1	13
Mark Pembroke	1(5)	0	0	0	0
Jason Roach	16(3)	7	0	0	28
Wes Rogers	12(3)	1	0	0	4
Robert Russell	8(5)	4	10	0	36
Ian Sinfield	23	4	0	0	16
Kris Smith	21(1)	5	7	0	34
Darren Speakman	(1)	0	0	0	0
Ryan Stazicker	4(2)	1	0	0	4
Hugh Thorpe	18(2)	8	0	0	32
Danny Tyrell	4	1	0	0	4
Andrew Wallace	(1)	0	0	0	0
Steve Warburton	3	0	0	0	0
Rob Whittaker	6(13)	1	0	0	4
Craig Wingfield	6(10)	1	1	0	6

Season 2005

Player	Appearances	Tries	Goals	Drop-Goals	Points
Phil Anderton	2	0	0	0	0
Warren Ayres	3(15)	1	1	0	6
Danny Barton	5(6)	0	0	0	0
Marlon Billy	27	26	0	0	104
Mick Coates	26(1)	8	3	0	38
Andy Crabtree	5(7)	1	0	0	4
Ben Cramant	1(2)	0	0	0	0
Wayne English	27	25	0	0	100
Craig Farrimond	1(5)	1	0	0	4
Lee Gardner	1(4)	1	0	0	4
Neil Hayden	(1)	0	0	0	0
Danny Heaton	27(1)	12	0	0	48
Ian Hodson	2(2)	0	0	0	0
Chris Irwin	10(1)	6	0	0	24
Phil Joseph	29	11	1	0	46
Matt Leigh	4(3)	1	0	0	4
Dave Llewellyn	3	2	0	0	8
Lee Marsh	27	20	114	2	310
Chris Maye	24	17	0	0	68
Alex Muff	1(1)	0	0	0	0
Stuart Oldham	22(1)	7	0	0	28
Ian Parry	4(11)	5	0	0	20
Safraz Patel	(5)	2	0	0	8
Lee Patterson	30	21	0	0	84
Wes Rogers	25(1)	2	0	0	8
Rob Russell	12(11)	2	0	0	8
Ian Sinfield	20(6)	4	0	0	16
Kris Smith	5(7)	1	2	0	8
Paul Southern	16(2)	2	0	0	8
Darren Speakman	1(2)	0	0	0	0
Hugh Thorpe	2	0	0	0	0
Ian Watson	22(2)	4	3	0	22
Rob Whittaker	6(22)	0	0	0	0

Season 2006

Player	Appearances	Tries	Goals	Drop-Goals	Points
Danny Aboushakra	4(5)	0	0	0	0
Paul Alcock	8(2)	4	0	0	16
David Alstead	23(3)	8	0	0	32
Dave Ashton	15	9	0	0	36
Marlon Billy	32	12	0	0	48
Mick Coates	10(2)	3	1	0	14
Andy Crabtree	9(6)	0	4	0	8
Dave Cunliffe	1(3)	0	0	0	0
Wayne English	33(1)	14	0	0	56
Craig Farrimond	3(2)	1	0	0	4
Keiron Hersnip	(6)	0	0	0	0
Chris Hough	7(4)	4	19	1	55
Jordan James	4(2)	0	0	0	0
Bruce Johnson	19(4)	5	0	0	20
Dave Llewellyn	11(2)	2	0	0	8
Lee Marsh	18(1)	7	41	2	112
Richard Marshall	22(5)	1	0	0	4
Steve McCurrie	8(8)	2	0	0	8
Liam McGovern	25(5)	3	38	0	88
Martin Moana	30	19	0	0	76
Chris Morley	16(11)	4	0	0	16
Kyle Neal	1(2)	0	0	0	0
Dave Newton	16(4)	0	0	0	0
Stuart Oldham	8(1)	2	0	0	8
Ian Parry	2(26)	2	0	0	8
Safraz Patel	1(6)	1	0	0	4
Dean Rhodes	(1)	0	0	0	0
Wes Rogers	9(1)	0	0	0	0
Andy Saywell	30(1)	26	0	0	104
Ian Sinfield	13(14)	5	0	0	20
Kris Smith	20	4	23	0	62
Mike Stout	10(10)	7	0	0	28
Tama Wakelin	1(1)	1	0	0	4
Ian Watson	12	3	5	0	22
Rob Whittaker	4(1)	0	0	0	0
Phil Wood	16	7	0	0	28
Darren Woods	14	16	0	0	64

Season 2007

Player	Appearances	Tries	Goals	Drop-Goals	Points
Danny Aboushakra	2(4)	0	0	0	0
Paul Alcock	15(2)	4	0	0	16
Craig Ashall	20(3)	6	1	0	26
Dave Ashton	9(1)	2	0	0	8
David Bates	9(4)	4	0	0	16
Marlon Billy	25	12	0	0	48
Adam Bowman	4	0	0	0	0
Mark Brocklehurst	14	4	0	0	16
Matt Bryers	3(10)	0	0	0	0
Sean Conway	2	0	0	0	0
Rob Draper	4(1)	0	0	0	0
Jay Duffy	5(3)	2	0	0	8
Wayne English	28(1)	8	0	0	32
Craig Farrimond	4(7)	0	0	0	0
Dean Gorton	14(1)	5	0	0	20
Gareth Hayes	14(15)	2	0	0	8
Chris Hough	8(9)	2	3	0	14
Chris Hull	8	4	0	0	16
Bruce Johnson	18(3)	4	0	0	16
Rob Line	16(8)	6	0	0	24
Lee Marsh	19(4)	7	61	0	150
Richard Marshall	1(4)	0	0	0	0
Steve McCurrie	(4)	0	0	0	0
Liam McGovern	25(2)	3	43	3	101
Martin Moana	22(8)	10	0	0	40
Chris Morley	11(10)	3	0	0	12
Dave Newton	10(10)	2	0	0	8
Mark Ogden	5	1	2	0	8
Andy Saywell	22	21	0	0	84
Adam Sharples	(2)	0	0	0	0
Mike Smith	19(4)	3	0	0	12
John Walker	2(1)	2	0	0	8
Kash Watkins	3	1	0	0	4
Desi Williams	13	7	0	0	28
Ben Williamson	3(3)	1	0	0	4
Phil Wood	26(2)	11	0	0	44
Darren Woods	12(1)	12	0	0	48

Season 2008

Player	Appearances	Tries	Goals	Drop-Goals	Points
Craig Ashall	12(6)	3	0	0	12
Rob Ball	9(7)	2	0	0	8
Darren Bamford	15(4)	6	2	0	28
David Bates	(6)	1	0	0	4
Adam Bibey	(4)	0	0	0	0
Marlon Billy	23	18	0	0	72
Adam Bowman	2	0	0	0	0
Chris Brand	4(1)	2	8	0	24
Matt Bryers	1(1)	0	0	0	0
Paul Crook	3(2)	0	6	0	12
Dayne Donoghue	3	1	0	0	4
Wayne English	16	6	0	0	24
Chris Frodsham	10(3)	2	1	0	10
Darren Gibson	13(3)	3	0	0	12
Dean Gorton	21	7	0	0	28
Barry Hamilton	11	3	0	0	12
Richie Hawkyard	22(3)	3	47	0	106
Gareth Hayes	5(14)	3	0	0	12
Ian Hodson	5	0	0	0	0
Chris Hull	14(3)	6	0	0	24
Gary Hulse	24(3)	5	0	0	20
Bruce Johnson	16(11)	3	0	0	12
Richard Jones	(2)	0	0	0	0
Rob Line	26(1)	2	0	0	8
Liam McGovern	15(6)	7	21	2	72
Ryan Mirfield	2	0	0	0	0
Martin Moana	18(12)	11	0	0	44
Chris Morley	2	0	0	0	0
Paul Raftrey	1(2)	0	0	0	0
Neil Rigby	24(2)	2	0	0	8
Andy Saywell	17	9	0	0	36
Mike Smith	(6)	0	0	0	0
Gary Sykes	23(2)	5	5	0	30
Chris Tyrer	8(8)	0	0	0	0
Mike Wainwright	5	0	0	0	0
Ben Williamson	7	2	0	0	8
Phil Wood	12(5)	4	0	0	16
Dave York	1(3)	0	0	0	0

Appendix E: Whatever happened to XIII Swinton players?
The careers of thirteen players after leaving the Lions

Over the past 10 years whilst Wayne English has remained at Swinton most other players at the club have either moved elsewhere or retired from the professional game altogether. The following is an account of what happened to thirteen former Swinton players after they left the Lions.

Peter Cannon played for Swinton with distinction in two spells having been previously at St Helens. He first signed for the Lions in June 1995 and enjoyed a successful time at Gigg Lane leaving the club in 1998. In his second spell from 2002 to 2004, Peter was club captain for a period at Park Lane and served the club well mainly playing at hooker and distributing the ball effectively from dummy-half. In total, he made 134 appearances for Swinton including 19 as substitute, scoring 39 tries. After leaving Swinton, Peter played at Warrington RUFC and then joined the coaching team at Crosfields ARLFC. In 2008, Peter was named club captain of Rugby League Conference side Lymm Wolves scoring 14 tries in 11 appearances in the inaugural season and even got his good friend Adrian Morley to help out at the club.

Sean Casey signed for Swinton in December 1996 from Whitehaven having played previously at St Helens where he had vied for the number nine shirt with Keiron Cunningham. Sean is a very competitive player who also captained the Lions to great effect at Gigg Lane mainly from the loose-forward position. In total, he made 102 appearances plus 1 as substitute for the Lions scoring 38 tries, 5 goals and 9 drop-goals in a four-season spell from 1997 to 2000. After leaving the Lions due to injury, Sean played rugby union for Liverpool-St Helens and on one occasional scored a memorable try at Macclesfield where Swinton duo Martin Birkett and Gavin Price-Jones had played during the close-season in the mid-1990s.

Andy Coley signed for the Lions in January 1997 from Warrington amateur club Laporte ARLFC as a second-row forward with devastating strength and speed. He broke into the first-team in 1997 and it became apparent immediately that he had a great future ahead of him in the game. In total, he played four seasons at Swinton scoring 20 tries in 48 appearances plus 16 as substitute limited by a cruciate ligament injury sustained in 2000, but he still managed to lay the foundation for future England appearances. After leaving the Lions, Andy signed for Salford making 112 Super League appearances plus 34 as substitute between 2001 and 2007 (not including the 2003 season in National League One) scoring 34 tries, where his overall speed and rugby skills were not fully utilised as a prop. In 2008, he finally fulfilled his true potential when he signed for Wigan where he made 30 appearances scoring 4 tries.

Andy Craig signed initially for the Lions in December 1996 from Wigan where he had scored two tries in the 1996 season. He had two successful seasons at Gigg Lane in the centres and at half-back, appearing in 56 games plus 3 as substitute scoring 27 tries and 9 goals. Andy then returned to Super League in 1999 with Halifax where he played 20 times scoring a single try and three goals. He was back at Swinton in 2000 teaming up with Mike Gregory who was also the Scotland Rugby League assistant-coach at the time and played a further 26 times scoring 16 tries for the Lions before deciding to play rugby union in the winter for Orrell. After a brief spell at Widnes in 2001, he then returned to rugby union rejoining Orrell on a permanent basis before moving to Glasgow and eventually Leeds Tykes. By 2002, Andy was representing Scotland at rugby union having played previously for Scotland at rugby league in 1999. He became the first former Swinton player to make this journey from the XIII-a-side game to the XV-a-side game at international level. In an ironic twist, towards the end of his playing career he joined Sedgley Park at Park Lane where the Lions are now based.

Dale Holdstock became a dependable back-row forward during the uncertain times of 2002. Hull-born Dale is the son of former Hull Kingston Rovers player Roy Holdstock and in spite of this origin he played initially for the St Helens Academy. In a brief, but memorable, stint at Swinton between 2001 and 2002 he played 36 times plus 6 as substitute scoring 7 tries and was popular for his hard working displays and rapport with the supporters. Dale eventually played for his home-town club, Hull Kingston Rovers and ultimately came back to haunt the Lions playing superbly well for Sheffield Eagles against Swinton in the 2006 Grand Final.

Chris Hough will be always remembered in Swinton folklore as well as in the history books as the first player to score a golden point in professional British rugby league when the Lions beat Celtic Crusaders in 2006 Elimination Play-off. He first joined the Lions in 2003 as a creative scrum-half and then moved onto Doncaster and eventually Blackpool Panthers before returning to the Lions in 2006. Chris is a hugely likeable person who would often be seen after the game with his family. In 2008, he joined Rochdale Hornets and helped out in the coaching side at Spotland. He has also enjoyed playing in the amateur ranks recently for Rochdale Mayfield ARLFC.

Richard Marshall was a consistent performer at prop in Super League between 1996 and 2005 and played for Halifax, Huddersfield, London and Leigh. He joined Swinton in 2006 and played 22 times plus five as substitute scoring one try. The 2007 season was blighted by injury and he made only one start plus four as substitute and consequently retired from playing before the end of that season. Richard helped out with the coaching at Park Lane using his vast experience for the benefit of the entire team. In 2008, he left Swinton for a coaching position at Warrington Wolves where he has been working mainly with the Academy players.

Mick Nanyn first appeared in the professional game for Swinton in 1999 and eventually made 71 appearances plus 10 as substitute mainly in the centres scoring 40 tries and 152 goals. He still holds jointly (with Greg Pearce) the Swinton record for points in a match with 30 against York in March 2001. Mick is the son of former Wigan player Mick Nanyn (senior) who featured in the second-row for at Central Park from 1979 to 1983 after signing from Saddleworth Ranger ARLFC. After leaving Swinton, Mick (junior) has played at Whitehaven, Rochdale Hornets, Widnes and Oldham performing consistently well at each club. He was rewarded with selection in the Scotland national team for the 2008 Rugby League World Cup in Australia featuring in every match against France, Fiji and Tonga and subsequently signed for Harlequins Rugby League for the 2009 season.

Jason Roach had a phenomenal try-scoring record at Swinton after first signing for the Lions in June 1995 from St Helens. In three spells at Swinton from 1995 to 1996, in 2000 and from 2002 to 2004 he made 139 appearances for Swinton including 13 as substitute, scoring 94 tries playing on the wing and at full-back. Also, he scored 3 goals for the Lions, all against Chorley in April 1996. In addition, Jason played in Super League for Castleford and Warrington in between spells at the Lions as well briefly at Whitehaven before ending his playing career at Barrow and Blackpool Panthers in all scoring 19 tries in Super League and over 100 tries in the National League. Furthermore, he played rugby union for Orrell and Birmingham-Solihull. Since retiring, Jason has been coaching Haydock ARLFC and in 2008 appeared in the St Helens team of legends for charity along with other former Swinton players including Gary Forber, Paul Loughlin, Chris Morley and Ian Pickavance.

Kris Smith first arrived in professional rugby league with one-off substitute appearances for both London Broncos and Halifax in 2001 having played in the Leeds Academy. The majority of his playing career has been at Swinton from 2003 to 2006 in the back-row and occasionally at stand-off, but his career has been hampered by persistent injuries. In total, he made 53 appearances plus 18 as substitute for the Lions scoring 12 tries and 33 goals but the 2006 Grand Final was the last game for Kris in Swinton colours. In 2007 Kris played a further 10 times for Oldham before retiring altogether from playing to coach at Eccles ARLFC. In October 2008, Kris achieved international media attention when he started dating Australian superstar and X-factor judge Dannii Minogue.

Paul Smith made a big impression at Swinton when he burst into the first team squad in 1999. In three seasons with the Lions he played mainly in the second row and scored 35 tries from 54 appearances plus 15 as substitute. Paul is tough in defence and always joined the attacking line well and consequently scores a lot of tries for a back-row forward. Such rave performances meant that other clubs would become interested and in 2002 he left the Lions to join Rochdale Hornets where he stayed for two seasons. Paul then moved to Huddersfield Giants in Super League scoring 13 tries in 52 appearance plus 17 as substitute in a three-year spell. In 2007 he moved again, this time to Halifax making the head-lines for some more fine performances as well as for having his nose broken accidentally by his wife while on honeymoon.

Phil Veivers is a genuine legend who first signed for St Helens in September 1984 and played at Knowsley Road until 1996. He played a total of 381 games for Saints scoring 98 tries and five drop-goals. He joined Huddersfield in 1998 before moving to Swinton in the 2001 season playing 20 times plus 1 as substitute scoring 5 tries influencing games effectively from loose forward. He coached the Lions in 2002 after the departure of Tony Humphries but left the club at the end of the season. Phil gained further coaching experience at both Huddersfield and Bradford and in May 2006 joined the coaching staff at Wigan.

Ian Watson is a former Swinton ball-boy at Station Road who first joined the Lions on loan from Salford in January 1998 before signing permanently and has also had another spell with the Lions. Ian began his playing career at Eccles ARLFC and since signing professionally as a scrum-half his career has been typical of the modern day rugby league player in terms of changing clubs on a regular basis. In total, Ian has played for eight clubs namely Salford, Workington Town, Swinton, Oldham, Rochdale Hornets, Widnes, Halifax and Leigh. Even so Ian has played mostly for the Lions between 1998 to 2000 and 2005 to 2006 including an unbroken run of 90 consecutive appearances in his first spell at the club.

Ian Watson: playing career by club 1995 to 2008

Club	Appearances	Substitute	Tries	Goals	Drops	Total
Leigh	27	0	5	62	2	146
Halifax	25	5	3	9	1	31
Oldham	20	0	6	5	7	41
Rochdale	32	0	7	27	6	88
Salford	35	25	8	27	9	95
Swinton	126	2	30	161	14	456
Widnes	37	4	0	73	2	148
Workington	4	1	1	15	0	34
Total	**306**	**37**	**60**	**379**	**41**	**1,039**

It's hard being a full-back from Rochdale:
Wayne English is tackled by a Rochdale Hornets player at Park Lane, 13 February 2005

Appendix F: Wayne English's top ten matches

Match One
Swinton Lions versus Waterhead
Gigg Lane, Bury
Challenge Cup – Round Three
1 February 2000

Swinton Lions	74 – 1 Number	Waterhead
English	1	Parkinson
Roach	2	Thewliss
Bateman	3	Lord
Coussons	4	Greener
Billy	5	Campbell
Craig	6	Perks
Watson	7	Wood
Noels	8	Howe
Highton	9	McAndrew
Barrow, T	10	Conway
Coley	11	Milne
Smith	12	Eastwood
Casey	13	Pearson
Henare	14	Standring
Pickavance	15	Bradshaw
Neill	16	Agard
Barrow, P	17	McDonald

Scorers: Coussons (2), Craig (2), Barrow, P (2), Henare (2), Casey, Highton, Smith, English, Barrow, T, Coley, Bateman, Roach scored the tries plus Watson (5) goals for the Lions; and Perks drop-goal (1) for Waterhead.
Attendance: 588
Half-time: 34-0
Newspaper: Swinton's sweet 16 tries (*Independent*) Dave Hadfield
Referee: Karl Kirkpatrick (Warrington)

Match Two
Swinton Lions versus Featherstone Rovers
Moor Lane, Kersal
Challenge Cup – Fifth Round
2 March 2003

Swinton Lions	32 – 10	Featherstone Rovers
	Number	
English	1	Graham
	2	Stokes
Roach		
Tassell	3	O'Meara
Hassan	4	McNally
Thorpe	5	Flynn
Hough	6	Agar
Cannon	7	Briggs
Leatham	8	Molyneux
Barrowclough	9	Chapman
Knox	10	Jowitt
Wingfield	11	Brown
Ellison	12	Rice
Russell	13	Seal
Hudson	14	Whiting
Johnson	15	Bailey
Cheetham	16	Dickens
Cushion	17	Tonks

Scorers: Hassan, English, Johnson, Thorpe, Knox, Cushion scored the tries plus Hough (3) goals and drop-goal (2) for the Lions; O'Meara and Brown scored the tries and Dickens (1) goal for Rovers.
Attendance: 1,092
Half-time: 11-4
Newspaper: Gritty Lions head for showdown (*Advertiser*) Claire Mooney
Referee: Peter Taberner (Wigan)

Match Three
Swinton Lions versus Wigan Warriors
JJB Stadium, Wigan
Challenge Cup - Quarter Final
16 March 2003

Swinton Lions	12 – 70	Wigan Warriors
	Number	
English	1	Radlinski
Roach	2	Dallas
Tassell	3	Aspinwall
Hassan	4	Hodgson
Thorpe	5	Ainscough
Hough	6	Robinson
Cannon	7	Lam
Leathem	8	Sculthorpe
Barraclough	9	Newton
Knox	10	Smith, C
Wingfield	11	Hock
Cushion	12	Johnson
Russell	13	O'Loughlin
Hudson	14	Bibey
Johnson	15	Smith, M
Cheetham	16	Wild
Ellison	17	O'Neill

Scorers: Russell, Leathem scored the tries plus Hough (2) goals for the Lions; Dallas (2), Robinson, Hock, Johnson, Ainscough, Hodgson, Bibey, Smith M., Aspinwall, O'Loughlin, Lam scored the tries plus O'Neil (7) and Robinson (2) goals for the Warriors.
Attendance: 5,114
Half-time: 6-30
Newspaper: Lions' spirit stands out (*The Guardian*) Andy Wilson
Referee: Karl Kirkpatrick (Warrington)

Match Four
Swinton Lions versus York City Knights
Moor Lane, Kersal
National League Two
17 August 2003

Swinton Lions	38 – 16	York City Knights
	Number	
English	1	Brown
Thorpe	2	Godfrey
Roach	3	Hallas
Tassell	4	Callaghan
Hudson	5	Kama
Hough	6	Hughes
Bithell	7	Brough
Tyres	8	Hayes
Cannon	9	Jackson
Knox	10	Helme
Gorski	11	Ramsden
Barton	12	Smith
Gallagher	13	Krause
Saunders	14	Deakin
Smith	15	Molloy
Roe	16	Cain
Loughlin	17	Forsyth

Scorers: Roach (3), Hudson (2), Tassell, Loughlin scored the tries plus goals Hough (4) and drop-goals (2) for the Lions; and Hughes, Kama (2) scored the tries plus Brough (2) goals for the Knights.
Attendance: 551
Half-time: 22-6
Newspaper: Lions maul Knights (*League Express*) Ian Rigg
Referee: Steve Addy (Huddersfield)

Match Five
Nation League Two Select versus New Zealand 'A'
Cougar Park, Keighley
International Tour
22 October 2003

National League Two Select	27 – 8 Number	New Zealand 'A'
(Swinton Lions) **English**	1	Fisiiahi
(Chorley Lynx) **McCulley**	2	Tupou
(Keighley Cougars) **Foster, M**	3	Taumoli
(Keighley Cougars) **Foster, D**	4	Vaa'sa
(Gateshead Thunder) **Barnett**	5	Apuula
(Swinton Lions) **Hough**	6	Bailey
(Keighley Cougars) **Firth**	7	Buckingham
(Keighley Cougars) **Stephenson**	8	Tuakura
(York City Knights) **Jackson**	9	Beyers
(York City Knights) **Sozi**	10	Mackie
(Sheffield Eagles) **Raleigh**	11	Royal
(Hunslet Hawks) **Freeman**	12	Poka
(Keighley Cougars) **Ramshaw**	13	Limmer
(Sheffield Eagles) **Stringer**	14	Herangi
(Keighley Cougars) **Sinfield**	15	Faitala
(London Skolars) **Jonker**	16	Pelenise
(Keighley Cougars) **Hoyle**	17	Pau

Scorers: Barnet, McCully and Hough scored the tries plus Hough goals (7) and drop-goal (1) for the NL2 team and Apuula (2) scored the tries for New Zealand 'A'.
Attendance: 1,000 estimated
Penalty Count: 18-7
Newspaper: Roe: Kiwis lack fitness and discipline (PA Sport) Ian Laybourn
Referee: Ronnie Laughton (Barnsley)

Match Six
Swinton Lions versus Workington Town
Park Lane, Whitefield
National League Two
10 April 2005

Swinton Lions	56-18	Workington Town
	Number	
English	1	Chilton
Irwin	2	Woodcock
Patterson	3	Frazer
Maye	4	Hetherington
Billy	5	Wilson
Coates	6	Kiddie
Watson	7	Manihera
Southern	8	Beamont
Joseph	9	Burns
Rogers	10	Burgess
Heaton	11	Tuimualuga
Russell	12	Limmer
Marsh	13	Robinson
Ayres	14	Johnson
Smith	15	Lavulavu
Sinfield	16	Armstrong
Whittaker	17	Caton

Scorers: English (3), Joseph, Southern, Coates (2), Patterson (2), Billy scored the tries plus Marsh (8) goals for the Lions; Limmer, Kiddie and Manihera scored the tries plus Manihera (3) goals for Town.
Attendance: 602
Half-time: 32-6
Newspaper: *League Express* man-of-the-match: Lee Patterson
Referee: Jamie Leahy (Dewsbury)

Match Seven
Featherstone Rovers versus Swinton Lions
Post Office Road, Featherstone
Elimination Semi-Final
24 September 2006

Featherstone Rovers	14-27 Number	Swinton Lions
Larvin	1	English
Kirmond	2	Saywell
McHugh	3	Woods
Cardoza	4	Alcock
Wray	5	Billy
Blakeway	6	Moana
Speak	7	McGovern
Tonks	8	Johnson
Swinson	9	Wood
Dickens	10	Newton
Dooler	11	Smith
Houston	12	Sinfield
Hughes, C	13	Marsh
Hughes, P	14	Hough
L'Anson	15	Morley
Moss	16	McCurrie
Birchall	17	Parry

Scorers: Alcock, Saywell (2), Woods, Smith scored the tries for the Lions plus Hough (3) goals and Marsh (1) drop-goal for the Lions; Dickens (2) scored the tries plus Dickens (3) goals for Rovers.
Attendance: 1,205
Half-time: 2-8
Newspaper: *League Express* man-of-the-match: Lee Marsh
Referee: Peter Taberner (Wigan)

Match Eight
Celtic Crusaders versus Swinton Lions
Brewery Field, Bridgend
Final Eliminator
1 October 2006

Celtic Crusaders	26-27	Swinton Lions
	Number	
Duggan	1	English
Epton	2	Saywell
James	3	Woods
Quinn	4	Alcock
Hill	5	Billy
Young	6	Moana
Van Dijk	7	Hough
Dean	8	Johnson
Ryan	9	Wood
Price	10	Newton
Barton	11	Smith
Beasley	12	Sinfield
Wyatt	13	Marsh
Morgan	14	McGovern
Davies, G	15	Morley
Davies, H	16	McCurrie
Seibold	17	Parry

Scorers: Hill (2), Beasley, Ryan and Duggan scored the tries and van Dijk (3) scored the goals for the Crusaders; Alcock, Woods, Marsh (2), McGovern scored the tries plus Hough, Marsh, McGovern (1) goal each and Hough the golden point drop goal for the Lions.
Attendance: 687
Half-time: 10-10 (26-26 after 80 minutes and the same after extra-time)
Newspaper: *League Express* man-of-the-match: Chris Hough
Referee: Julian King (St Helens)

Match Nine
Sheffield Eagles versus Swinton Lions
Halliwell-Jones Stadium, Warrington
The Grand Final
8 October 2006

Sheffield Eagles	35-10 Number	Swinton Lions
Woodcock	1	English
Hurst	2	Saywell
Walker	3	Woods
Ford	4	Alstead
Worrincy	5	Billy
Lindsay	6	Moana
Brown	7	Hough
Howieson	8	Johnson
Pickering	9	Wood
Stringer	10	Newton
Hay	11	Smith
Holdstock	12	Sinfield
Smith	13	Marsh
Poucher	14	McGovern
Ostler	15	Morley
Dickinson	16	Aboushakra
Sovatbua	17	Parry

Scorers: Worrincy (2), Linsdsay, Woodcock, Walker, Hay scored the tries plus Woodcock (5) goals and Brown (1) drop-goal for the Eagles and Saywell, Alstead scored the tries and McGovern (1) goal for the Lions.
Attendance: 13,024 (overall total for the three Grand Finals)
Half-time: 16-4
Newspaper: *League Express* man-of-the-match: Wayne English
Referee: Peter Taberner (Wigan)

Match Ten
Swinton Lions versus Hunslet Hawks
Park Lane, Whitefield
National League Two
3 August 2008

Swinton Lions	36-20	Hunslet Hawks
	Number	
English	1	Larvin
Saywell	2	Aitken
Hull	3	Robinson
Gorton	4	Cook
Billy	5	Childs
Hawkyard	6	Maloney
McGovern	7	Moxon
Line	8	Freeman
Sykes	9	Wainhouse
Johnson	10	Walkin
Rigby	11	Bovill
Wainwright	12	Blanchard
Moana	13	Young
Hulse	14	Chapman
Bamford	15	Hasty
Bates	16	Thewliss
Hayes	17	Helme

Scorers: English, Billy, Moana, McGovern, Gorton, Bamford scored the tries plus Hawkyard (2) and McGovern (4) goals for the Lions; Chapman, Young and Aitken scored the tries and Young (2) goals for the Hawks.
Attendance: 335
Half-time: 16-12
Newspaper: *League Express* man-of-the-match: Wayne English
Referee: Jamie Leahy (Dewsbury)

Appendix G: Wayne English's Swinton Lions XIII: 1998 to 2008
Wayne has named the best Swinton XIII in his time with the club. The only condition was that he was selected in the full back position.

1. Full-back: Wayne ENGLISH
2. Right wing: Richard HENARE
3. Right centre: Mick NANYN
4. Left centre: Kris TASSELL
5. Left wing: Marlon BILLY
6. Stand-off: Andy CRAIG
7. Scrum-half: Ian WATSON
8. Open-side prop: Simon KNOX
9. Hooker: Peter CANNON
10. Blind-side prop: Lee HANSEN
11. Second row: Paul SMITH
12. Second row: Andy COLEY
13. Loose forward: Phil VEIVERS

Appendix H: Wayne English's All-time World Rugby League XIII
Wayne has named his all-time world Rugby League XIII. This time no conditions or restrictions were attached.

1. Full-back: Ken GOWERS
2. Right wing: Martin OFFIAH
3. Right centre: Mal MANINGA
4. Left centre: Alan BUCKLEY
5. Left wing: Jason ROBINSON
6. Stand-off: Darren LOCKYER
7. Scrum-half: Andrew JOHNS
8. Open-side prop: Shane WEBAKE
9. Hooker: Keiron CUNNINGHAM
10. Blind-side prop: Iafaet PALEAASINA
11. Second row: Gordon TALLIS
12. Second row: Adrian MORLEY
13. Loose forward: Ellery HANLEY

Subscribers

The following people are subscribers to this book and helped make it all possible.

Chris Allen ■ Dave Arnold ■ Graham Berry ■ Wayne Berry ■ Neil Beswick ■ Nigel Boothman ■ Ray Bowdler ■ Sarah Brittain ■ Alicia Brookes ■ Sue Buckley ■ Mike Caine ■ Paul Catchpole ■ Barbara S Cathcart ■ Ken Chichester ■ Sam Collier ■ John Corcoran ■ Alan Cresswell ■ Ray Cresswell ■ Mike Dagnan ■ Paul Davidson ■ Lol Duffy ■ Rob Dunford ■ Jason Ellar ■ Mitchel Ellar ■ Denise English ■ Wayne English ■ Christine Fairchild ■ Malcolm Ferguson ■ Barbara Gettins ■ Charlotte Gettins ■ Christopher Gettins ■ Claire Gettins ■ Colin Gettins ■ Pete Green ■ Alan Greenall ■ Tony Greenhalgh ■ Rhys Griffiths ■ Nick Hill ■ Steve Hinds ■ Garry Jackson ■ George Jackson ■ Ian Jackson ■ James Jackson ■ Thomas Jackson ■ Arthur Johnson ■ Ben Anthony Johnson ■ Stephen Johnson ■ Lee Kirkman ■ Olwyn Kirkman ■ Vincent Kirkman ■ Cliff Lenord ■ Lee Marshall ■ Muriel Marsland ■ Simon Mather ■ Martin McDonough ■ Bryce MacDonald ■ Stuart MacDonald ■ Val MacDonald ■ Anna Mooney ■ Claire Mooney ■ Joe Mooney ■ Pete Mooney ■ Sandra Nicholson ■ Emily Parker ■ Jamie Parker ■ Stephen Parker ■ Tracey Parker ■ Yvonne Parker ■ Angel Parr ■ Pauline Pearson ■ Angela Poole ■ Emily Poole ■ Phil Poole ■ Sandra Preston ■ Wayne Rashman ■ Mark Richardson ■ Ian Rigg ■ David J Roberts ■ Jill Roberts ■ Robert Small ■ Angela Smith ■ Keith J Smith ■ Rick Smith ■ John Spellman ■ Mark Stevens ■ Angela Sulcas ■ Bill Sutton ■ Betty Taylor ■ Richard Taylor ■ John Thomason ■ Paul Thomason ■ Mark Tonge ■ Chris Tyldesley ■ Kath Tyldesley ■ Mike Tyldesley ■ Ian Wade ■ Peter Wakefield ■ Declan Walsh ■ Stephen M Wild ■ Myke Worthington ■ Diane Wragg

Two new books from London League Publications

All local lads
St Helens and Pilkington Recs RLFC
By Alex Service and Denis Whittle

The full story of the only works team ever to play in professional rugby league. From their early days in rugby union, to association football, St Helens Recs and then the post-war amateur Pilkington Recs, a fascinating tale of triumph, tragedy and survival against the odds.

Published in November 2008 at £13.95. Available direct from London League Publications Ltd for £13.00, post free. Credit card orders via www.llpshop.co.uk or by cheque payable to London League Publications Ltd to PO Box 10441, London E14 8WR. Or order from any bookshop for £13.95 (ISBN: 9781903659434)

Liverpool City RLFC
Rugby league in a football city
By Mike Brocken

Rugby league in Liverpool has a long history. Older fans have memories of visits to watch Liverpool Stanley before the war and Liverpool City in the 1950s and 1960s. This history of rugby league in Liverpool covers from the 1850s to the present day. It includes the first Liverpool City RLFC, Wigan Highfield and London Highfield, the forerunners to Liverpool Stanley RLFC, and the club after it moved to Huyton in 1969 until it was wound up in 1997.

Published in October 2008 at £14.95. Order from London League Publications for £14.00 post free. Credit card orders via www.llpshop.co.uk or by cheque payable to London League Publications Ltd to PO Box 10441, London E14 8WR. Or order from any bookshop for £14.95
(ISBN: 9781903659403)

A great book from London League Publications

Peter Fox
The players' coach

Peter Fox was involved in professional rugby league for almost 50 years. After playing for Sharlston Rovers, he had a 13 year playing career with Featherstone Rovers, Batley, Hull KR and Wakefield Trinity, he became one of British rugby league's most successful coaches. Highlights of his coaching career include:
- Coaching Great Britain and England, including beating the Australians in 1978
- Winning eight matches with Yorkshire
- Winning the Challenge Cup and promotion with **Featherstone Rovers**
- Winning the First Division title in 1980 and 1981 with **Bradford Northern**
- Winning promotion with **Bramley**
- Winning the Premiership, Yorkshire Cup and John Player Trophy

With a foreword by David Hinchliffe, this authorised biography, published in June 2008 and based on extensive interviews and research, gives the inside story of Peter's at times controversial rugby league career. It includes how he developed the teams he coached, and the players he signed. Every rugby league fan will find it of great interest.

Special offer for readers of this book: £14.00 post free (cover price £14.95). Credit card orders via www.llpshop.co.uk or from PO Box 10441, London E14 8WR (Cheques payable to London League Publications Ltd). The book can also be ordered from any bookshop at £14.95. (ISBN: 9781903659397)